First World War
and Army of Occupation
War Diary
France, Belgium and Germany

1 DIVISION
Headquarters, Branches and Services
Commander Royal Engineers
1 January 1915 - 30 April 1915

WO95/1244B

The Naval & Military Press Ltd
www.nmarchive.com
Published in association with The National Archives

Published by

The Naval & Military Press Ltd

Unit 10 Ridgewood Industrial Park,

Uckfield, East Sussex,

TN22 5QE England

Tel: +44 (0) 1825 749494

www.naval-military-press.com

www.nmarchive.com

This diary has been reprinted in facsimile from the original. Any imperfections are inevitably reproduced and the quality may fall short of modern type and cartographic standards.

© Crown Copyright
Images reproduced by permission of The National Archives, London, England, 2015.

Contents

Document type	Place/Title	Date From	Date To
Heading	1st Division C.R.E. From 1st Jan To 30th April 1915		
Heading	War Diary C.R.E. 1st Division January 1915		
War Diary	Bethune	01/01/1915	31/01/1915
Heading	Work Reports		
Miscellaneous	Summary Of Work Performed By R.E. Units 1st Division. From Midday 10 Jan 11 Jan	11/01/1915	11/01/1915
Miscellaneous	Summary Of Work Performed By R.E. Units 1st Division. From Midday 11 Jan To Midday 12 Jan	12/01/1915	12/01/1915
Miscellaneous	Summary Of Work Performed By R.E. Units 1st Division. From Midday 12 Jan To Midday 13 Jan	13/01/1915	13/01/1915
Miscellaneous	Summary Of Work Performed By R.E. Units 1st Division. From Midday 13jan To Midday 14 Jan	14/01/1915	14/01/1915
Miscellaneous	Summary Of Work Performed By R.E. Units 1st Division. From Midday 14 Jan To Midday 15 Jan	15/01/1915	15/01/1915
Miscellaneous	Summary Of Work Performed By R.E. Units 1st Division. From Midday 15 Jan To Midday 16 Jan	16/01/1915	16/01/1915
Miscellaneous	Summary Of Work Performed By R.E. Units 1st Division. From Midday 16 Jan To Midday 17 Jan	17/01/1915	17/01/1915
Miscellaneous	Summary Of Work Performed By R.E. Units 1st Division. From Midday 17jan To Midday 18 Jan	18/01/1915	18/01/1915
Miscellaneous	Summary Of Work Performed By R.E. Units 1st Division. From Midday 18jan To Midday 19 Jan	19/01/1915	19/01/1915
Miscellaneous	Summary Of Work Performed By R.E. Units 1st Division. From Midday 19 Jan To Midday 20 Jan	20/01/1915	20/01/1915
Miscellaneous	Summary Of Work Performed By R.E. Units 1st Division. From Midday 20 Jan To Midday 21 Jan	21/01/1915	21/01/1915
Miscellaneous	Summary Of Work Performed By R.E. Units 1st Division. From Midday 21jan To Midday 22	22/01/1915	22/01/1915
Miscellaneous	Summary Of Work Performed By R.E. Units 1st Division. From Midday 22 Jan To Midday 23 Jan	25/01/1915	25/01/1915
Miscellaneous	Summary Of Work Performed By R.E. Units 1st Division. From Midday 23 Jan To Midday 24 Jan	24/01/1915	24/01/1915
Miscellaneous	Summary Of Work Performed By R.E. Units 1st Division. From Midday 25 Jan To Midday 26 Jan	26/01/1915	26/01/1915
Miscellaneous	Summary Of Work Performed By R.E. Units 1st Division. From Midday 26jan To Midday 27 Jan	27/01/1915	27/01/1915
Miscellaneous	Summary Of Work Performed By R.E. Units 1st Division. From Midday 27 Jan To Midday 28 Jan	28/01/1915	28/01/1915
Miscellaneous	Summary Of Work Performed By R.E. Units 1st Division. From Midday 28th Jan To Midday 29th Jan	29/01/1915	29/01/1915
Miscellaneous	Summary Of Work Performed By R.E. Units 1st Division. From Midday 29th Jan To Midday 30th Jan	30/01/1915	30/01/1915
Miscellaneous	Summary Of Work Performed By R.E. Units 1st Division. From Midday 30th Jan To Midday 31st Jan	31/01/1915	31/01/1915
Miscellaneous	Summary of Work Performed By R.E. Units 1st Division. From Midday 31st Jan To Midday 1st Feb.	01/02/1915	01/02/1915
Heading	War Diary C.R.E. 1st Division February 1915		
War Diary	Bethune	01/02/1915	04/02/1915
War Diary	Marles	05/02/1915	28/02/1915
Heading	Work Reports Training Scheme		

Miscellaneous	Summary Of Work Performed By R.E. Units 1st Division. From Midday 1st Feb To Midday 2nd Feb	26/02/1915	26/02/1915
Miscellaneous	Summary Of Work Performed By R.E. Units 1st Division. From Midday 2nd Feb To Midday 3rd Feb.	03/02/1915	03/02/1915
Miscellaneous	Summary Of Work Performed By R.E. Units 1st Division. From Midday 28th Feb 1915 To Midday 1st March	01/03/1915	01/03/1915
Miscellaneous	1st Division No. 95 (G). Scheme Of Training And Of Organization For The First Division, During The Period When It Is In Reserve.	30/01/1915	30/01/1915
Miscellaneous	With Reference To Circular Memorandum, 1st Div. No. 95 The Following Additional Instructions Are Issued--	09/02/1915	09/02/1915
Miscellaneous	1st Division No 95 (G). C.R.E. 1st Divn	11/02/1915	11/02/1915
Miscellaneous	1st Divn No. 95 (G). 1st Guards Brigade.	11/02/1915	11/02/1915
Miscellaneous	1st Div. No. 95 (G). 2nd Infantry Brigade. 3rd Infantry Brigade	11/02/1915	11/02/1915
Miscellaneous	1st Division No. 131 (G). 1st D. E. (For Information).	13/02/1915	13/02/1915
Miscellaneous	Notes On Wire Entanglements.		
Heading	Follow of Appreciation		
Miscellaneous	1st Division No. 130 (G).	12/02/1915	12/02/1915
Miscellaneous	1st Division No. 130/2 (G).	11/02/1915	11/02/1915
Miscellaneous	1st Division No. 130 (G).		
Miscellaneous	1st Division No. 130/1 (G). G.O.C., R.A. 1st Division.	11/02/1915	11/02/1915
Heading	War Diary C.R.E. 1st Division March 1915		
War Diary	Hinges.	01/03/1915	25/03/1915
War Diary	Locon	26/03/1915	30/04/1915
Miscellaneous	A Form. Messages And Signals.		
Miscellaneous	C Form (Duplicate). Messages And Signals.		
Miscellaneous	A Form. Messages And Signals.		
Miscellaneous	Hd Qrs 1st D.E.		
Miscellaneous	A Form. Messages And Signals.		
Miscellaneous	Messages And Signals.		
Miscellaneous	A Form. Messages And Signals.		
Miscellaneous	O.C. Hampston Fmb Engine.		
Miscellaneous	A Form. Messages And Signals.		
Miscellaneous	Messages And Signals.		
Miscellaneous	1st Division Engineers Daily Progress Report From Mid-Day 30-4-15 To Mid-Day 1-5-15	30/04/1915	30/04/1915
Miscellaneous	1st Division Engineers Daily Progress Report From Mid-Day 29-04-15 To Mid-Day 30-04-15	29/04/1915	29/04/1915
Miscellaneous	1st Division Engineers Daily Progress Report From Mid-Day 28-4-15 To Mid-Day 29-4-15	28/04/1915	28/04/1915
Miscellaneous	1st Division Engineers Daily Progress Report From Mid-Day 27-4-15 To Mid-Day 28-4-15	27/06/1915	27/06/1915
Miscellaneous	1st Division Engineers Daily Progress Report From Mid-Day 26-4-15 To Mid-Day 27-4-15	26/04/1915	26/04/1915
Miscellaneous	1st Division Engineers Daily Progress Report From Mid-Day 25-4-15 To Mid-Day 26-4-15	25/04/1915	25/04/1915
Miscellaneous	Summary of Work Performed By R & E Units 1st Division.		
Miscellaneous	1st Division Engineers Daily Progress Report From Mid-Day 24-04-15 To Mid-Day 25-04-15	24/04/1915	24/04/1915
Miscellaneous	Summary of Work Performed by R & E Units 1st Division.		
Miscellaneous	1st Division Engineers Daily Progress Report From Mid-Day 23-04-15 To Mid-Day 24-04-15	23/04/1915	23/04/1915

Miscellaneous	1st Division Engineers Daily Progress Report		
Miscellaneous	1st Division Engineers Daily Progress Report From Mid-Day 22-04-15 To Mid-Day 23-04-15		
Miscellaneous	Summary Of Work Performed By R & E Units 1st Division		
Miscellaneous	1st Division Engineers Daily Progress Report From Mid-Day 21-04-15 To Mid-Day 22-04-15	21/04/1915	21/04/1915
Miscellaneous	Summary Of Work Performed By R & E Units 1st Division.		
Miscellaneous	1st Division Engineers Daily Progress Report From Mid-Day 20-04-15. To Mid Day 21-04-15	20/04/1915	20/04/1915
Miscellaneous	Summary Of Work Performed By R & E Units 1st Division.		
Miscellaneous	1st Division Engineers Daily Progress Report From Mid-Day 19-04-15 To Mid-Day 200416	19/04/1915	19/04/1915
Miscellaneous	1st Division Engineers Daily Progress Report From Mid-Day 18-04-15 To Mid-Day 19-04-15	18/04/1915	18/04/1915
Miscellaneous	Summary Of Work Performed By R & E. Units 1st Division.		
Miscellaneous	1st Division Engineers Daily Progress Report From Mid-Day 14-04-15 to Mid-Day 15-04-15	17/04/1915	17/04/1915
Miscellaneous	Summary Of Work Performed By R&E. Units 1st Division.		
Miscellaneous	1st Division Engineers Daily Progress Report From Mid-Day 16-04-15 To Mid-Day 17-04-15.	16/04/1915	16/04/1915
Miscellaneous	Summary Of Work Performed By R&E. Units 1st Division.		
Miscellaneous	1st Division Engineers Daily Progress Report From Mid-Day 15-04-15 To Mid Day 16-04-15	15/04/1915	15/04/1915
Miscellaneous	Summary Of Work Performed By R&E. Units 1st Division.		
Miscellaneous	1st Division Engineers Daily Progress Report From Mid-Day 14-4-15 To Mid-Day 15-04-15	14/04/1915	14/04/1915
Miscellaneous	Summary Of Work Performed By R&E. Units 1st Division.		
Miscellaneous	1st Division Engineers Daily Progress Report From Mid-Day 13-04-15. To Mid-Day 14-04-15.	13/04/1915	13/04/1915
Miscellaneous	Summary Of Work Performed By R&E. Units 1st Division.		
Miscellaneous	1st Division Engineers Daily Progress Report From Mid-Day 12-04-15 To Mid-Day 13-04-15	12/04/1915	12/04/1915
Miscellaneous	1st Division Engineers Daily Progress Report From Mid-Day 11-04-15 To Mid-Day 12-04-15	11/04/1915	11/04/1915
Miscellaneous	Summary Of Work Performed By R&E. Units 1st Division.		
Miscellaneous	1st Division Engineers Daily Progress Report From Mid-Day 10-04-15. To Mid-Day 11-04-15	10/04/1915	10/04/1915
Miscellaneous	Summary Of Work Performed By R&E. Units 1st Division.		
Miscellaneous	1st Division Engineers Daily Progress Report From Mid-Day 09-04-15 To Mid-Day 10-04-15	09/04/1915	09/04/1915
Miscellaneous	Summary Of Work Performed By R&E. Units 1st Division.		
Miscellaneous	1st Division Engineers Daily Progress Report From Mid-Day 08-04-15 To Mid-Day 09-04-15		

Miscellaneous	1st Division Engineers Daily Progress Report From Mid-Day 07-04-15 To Mid-Day 08-04-15	07/04/1915	07/04/1915
Miscellaneous	Summary Of Work Performed By R&E. Units 1st Division.		
Miscellaneous	1st Division Engineers Daily Progress Report From Mid-Day 06-04-15 To Mid-Day 07-04-15	06/04/1915	06/04/1915
Miscellaneous	Summary Of Work Performed By R&E. Units 1st Division.		
Miscellaneous	1st Division Engineers Daily Progress Report From Mid-Day 05-04-15 To Mid-Day 06-05-15	05/04/1915	05/04/1915
Miscellaneous	Summary Of Work Performed By R&E. Units 1st Division.		
Miscellaneous	1st Division Engineers Daily Progress Report From Mid-Day 04-04-15 To Mid-Day 05-04-15	04/04/1915	04/04/1915
Miscellaneous	Summary Of Work Performed By R&E. Units 1st Division.		
Miscellaneous	1st Division Engineers Daily Progress Report From Mid-Day 03-04-15 To Mid-Day 04-04-15	03/04/1915	03/04/1915
Miscellaneous	1st Division Engineers Daily Progress Report From Mid-Day 02-04-15 To Mid-Day 03-04-15	02/04/1915	02/04/1915
Miscellaneous	1st Division Engineers Daily Progress Report From Mid-Day 01-04-15 To Mid-Day 02-04-15	01/04/1915	01/04/1915
Miscellaneous	Summary Of Work Performed By R&E. Units 1st Division.		

1st Division

C. R E

From 1st Jan To 30th April 1915

WAR DIARY

C.R.E. 1st DIVISION

January

1915

Army Form C.2118.

Instructions regarding
War Diaries and Intelligence Summaries
are contained in F.S.Regns, Part II,
and the Staff Manual respectively.
Title pages will be prepared in manuscript.

WAR DIARY
or
INTELLIGENCE SUMMARY

H.Q. 1st DIVISIONAL ENGINEERS

(No 6) January 1915

Hour, date, place	Summary of Events and Information.	Remarks and references to Appendices
BETHUNE 1.1.15	6 am. Message to Rowland Co re special work	A 117
	7.30 C.R.E. to BEUVRY – Remained out all day visiting Field Companies and HdQrs of Brigades. During afternoon visited fire trenches S. of canal held by 2nd Brigade.	
	6.30 p Adjutant with Lt. ALEXANDER, Rowland Co. took over 200 civilians returned from Major TURNER re Indian troops for work on intermediate line. These did not commence till nearly midday & owing to shelling were unable to do much.	
	3.30 p 18w SR 90 asking for R.E. assistance for 1st Brigade towing but – now was available trench all companies being fully employed	p. 90
	6 p Report pr Brigade re state frailway line near PONT FIXE	A 118
	Report on General quarters of lines of work in canal & surrounding country	A 119
	6.15 p R29 to 2 W. Swt. asking for return of work per Cos ready but tomorrow	A 120
	7 p A 107 p.m. Rowland Co. reporting progress of work.	A 121
	7.30 p Instructions sent to Lt. ALEXANDER Rowland Co. to report at 4.15 p.m. tell. Known to take over charge of work on 2nd line	G 414
	1st Dist. G 414 received	

Army Form C.2118

Instructions regarding
War Diaries and Intelligence Summaries
are contained in F.S.Regns, Part II,
and the Staff Manual respectively.
Title pages will be prepared in manuscript.

War Diary
or
INTELLIGENCE SUMMARY

(2)

Hour, date, place	Summary of Events and Information.	Remarks and references to Appendices
2.1.15 6a	Things to 23rd Co re work for 1st Brigade	A 122
6.5.	MAJ. TURNER RE Indian Corps visited CRE with reference to the scheme of 2nd line defence – Points d'appui & Ports the place of continuous line. Adjutant rode out with MAJ. TURNER and various points out of LE TOURET and at "Turning fork" ½ mile E. of GORRE Church.	
11.	LT. ALEXANDER arrived to arrange to take over from Maj. Turner CRE visited 23rd Co. 2nd Bge HQ. – Then in justed with 1st Inland Co. on a traverse to defence line from to Gloucester HQ. Williams returned to 2nd Inf HQ to meet G.O.C. 1st Div. 1 Sect. Lolland Co. visited during day at STUDENT under orders of OC 26 Co. Messages received during day attached.	1st Corps RE 126, 8, RE 129 2nd Ind RE 11 & 18 RE Park No 26 1st Div. G #33
3.1.15 6.	CRE to go roads to 23rd Co. Selected point d'appui at X road B. PONT FIXE & go. It approved by B.C. 2nd Bris.? Back to 23 Co. – Then in justed until along intermediate line of defence on to 26 Co. Thence to 3rd Inf HQ at Inland Co. & Inland Co. & Infant Centre.	

Army Form C.2118

Instructions regarding
War Diaries and Intelligence Summaries
are contained in F.S.Regs., Part II.
and the Staff Manual respectively. Title pages will be prepared in manuscript.

War Diary
or
INTELLIGENCE SUMMARY

(3)

Hour, date, place	Summary of Events and Information.	Remarks and references to Appendices
3.1.15 (cont?)	Adjutant completed December War Diary - later rode to GORRE to examine flooded areas Tn. to 26 Co. and defent centre - Mentioned to 2nd Div. Factory re Machine & to see Maj. Turner, Indian Corps re floods.	A 125
8.40 a	Message to 1st Corps acknowledging receipt of warner wind pumps	A 123
	Message to CRE 2nd Divn. re railway & pumps	A 126
8.45	Message to 26 Co. asking to report re Pilastrine – (report in file)	
9—	Message to Holland Co. re emergency & till relief of Railway line near Pont Fixe.	A 127
11 a	G 442 from 1st Div. re area which is flooded near LE QUESNOY	G 442
	A 126 to 26 Co. asking re report on this.	A 128
2 p	Reply from Holland Co. to A2. A 127	A 113
3.30	I am G 453 saying that Inf.p. will relieve 1st Div. & responsibility for 2nd line of defence.	S 45-7
	A 130 to Holland to re-supply	A 130

Army Form C.2118

Instructions regarding
War Diaries and Intelligence Summaries
are contained in F.S.Regns., Part II,
and the Staff Manual respectively. Title pages will be prepared in manuscript.

War Diary or Intelligence Summary

Hour, date, place	Summary of Events and Information. (4)	Remarks and references to Appendices
3.1.15 (Cont.) 5.30p	Report on BLASTINE to 1st Division	A 131
	Report re flooded area at LE QUESNOY	A 132
6 p	Report & plan of trenches received from Cordand Co	A 114 & 116
7.30 p	1st Div. G.457 received	P 457
4.1.15		
8.15	C.R.E. to 23rd & 26th Cos. Inspected work in intermediate line & decided details of points d'appui at GIVENCHY and 1/2 mile E. of PONT FIXE. Adjutant to Railway Co's office to make arrangements for a standard rail Rlw. sent to GORRE to repair line near PONT FIXE. Then to Roland Co to see trial of WARNER pumps. Then to report centre	
8.30	Message to Div. Amm. Column re barbed wire	A 134
12.30	Message to 2nd Div. R.E. Co re change of quarters	A 135
	A 138 to R.E. Park asking to list of stores available at STRAZEELE	A 136
4.15	Reply from 1st Div. Army List	1st Park No 37
6 p	2nd Div. R.E. 45 received	2. Div. R.E. 45

Army Form C.2118

Instructions regarding
War Diaries and Intelligence Summaries
are contained in F.S.Regns, Part II,
and the Staff Manual respectively.
Title pages will be prepared in manuscript.

War Diary
or
INTELLIGENCE SUMMARY.

(5)

Hour, date, place		Summary of Events and Information.	Remarks and references to Appendices
4-1-15 (Cont.)	6.15	Message 23: CO 8 Norland re asking for further points of aim —	A 137 & 138
	7.30p	Instructions to Holland Co. re repairs to washing line	A 139
	5.15p	1st Bn. G 471 received.	F 471
		1st Bn. G 473 re sending an officer & N.C.O. to Stoner for instruction in use of portable searchlight.	F 473
	10h	A 140 Holland Co. re WAGNER & HAM GREEN pumps	A 140
5-1-15	8a	CRE & Adjutant to 26th; CO report centre (8 23rd Co. Afterwards went through all front line trenches held by SUSSEX & NORTHAMPTONS. S.J. examined Northumbld. examined approaches to machine gun emplacement on embankment which was recently captured by enemy.	
		CRE later attended conference at 2nd Brigade H.Q. of S.W. Brigadiers.	A 141
	8:am	Message Holland Co. re night Stoner to view portable searchlight	A 142
		A.142 Culvert 162 re 26 CO	Culvert 182
	8.30		
	11	CRE Culvert 162 re fuze by ALDIS	

Army Form C.2118.

Instructions regarding
War Diaries and Intelligence Summaries
are contained in F.S.Regns, Part II,
and the Staff Manual respectively. Title
pages will be prepared in manuscript.

War Diary
INTELLIGENCE SUMMARY
or

Hour, date, place		Summary of Events and Information.	Remarks and references to Appendices
5.1.15 (cont)	2.30	RR.134 from 1st Corps re. barbed wire for wire in 2nd line	RE 134
	7p	Circular IF 3 saying that 5000 fuse lighters will be delivered at ArmD factory tonight & 40000 more in a few days	Off. Intce 163
	7.30	Report re WARNER fuseups received from Intce Co.	A 118
6.1.15	8.15	CRE & Adjutant to ArmD factory where new fuse lighters were inspected. A number of fuses & sandbags were taken to 23rd Coy. Cas informants returned & took offices. MO of InfD and Co to SE	
		OME R for instruction. An hour was scarcely out OCS & Adjutant to HQ 2nd Bgde to state with fuse	
		2.30 to RHD of Sussex & Northampton Regiments	
		Back to 23rd Co - 11th Bde & Report centre	
		Kashmir Coy & 26th Coy.	
	1.30	IDI F.453	F 453
	4.15p	Mepho IE. 137 received	IE 137
	5.10	A145 (SECRET) to InfanD looking for report on Terminal Embankment passage to LA BASSEE	A145 (SECRET)

Army Form C.2118.

Instructions regarding
War Diaries and Intelligence Summaries
are contained in F.S.Regns, Part II,
and the Staff Manual respectively. Title pages will be prepared in manuscript.

War Diary
or
INTELLIGENCE SUMMARY

(7)

Hour, date, place	Summary of Events and Information.	Remarks and references to Appendices
6.1.15 (cont?) 6 p	Report from Latour Br. on handsomer pumps received. A 146 to 18 D.V. reporting that "Rees" pump is much superior to Warner pattern. 1st Div. 8501 received	A 146 8501
7.1.15 6.15 a	Detailed report re pumps to 5. Division	A 147
9 "	OC Adjutant to 23. Co. – Then F2. Brigh. H.Q. At which saw & have been made the day – Drove the m.g. emplacement on railway bridge – proposed road to the very bad western road to further reconnaissance. OC Adjutant the went to 1 Div. H.Q. & then to Givenchy to inspect work J. informed Col. re "keep" afterwards dismounted front near to Cuinchy dock – Returned via F. Brig., 23. Co. HQ, arrive a 2.6. Co.	
2 p	Pumps from OCS 2nd Ind. Cavalry Division asking for brushes & flares	OCS 2/ Ind. Cav. Div. No 10 A 148
5 p	Reply, to above asking to meeting	

Army Form C.2118.

Instructions regarding
War Diaries and Intelligence Summaries
are contained in F.S. Regns, Part II,
and the Staff Manual respectively. Title pages will be prepared in manuscript.

War Diary
or
INTELLIGENCE SUMMARY

Hour, date, place	Summary of Events and Information.	Remarks and references to Appendices
7.15 (Inst.) 5.15	Rept. from Island D. re. completion of repairs to railway line	A.124
7.30	1 Div. Order No. 51 received	1 Div. 51
11.15p	1 Div. S.A. 3 (SECRET) received	1 Div S.A. 3 (SECRET)
6.1.15 6.45a 11.	A 150 to 26 Co. ce HTM DAFER PUMP CRE of Indian Cavalry Divs. came to see CRE with ref. to supply of bombs — 2 supplement of Recce Troop (native). Proceeded with OBE Rajputana 4th Bde. Sialkot Brigde (they had taken over from 3rd Brigade) Afterwards CRE went with intent to inspect point of affairs being relieved by 26 Co. Park & Brig. A. 4th when Pt. 1 Div. was met — Then to 1" & 2" Bde & HQ. 925, 926, 630 to make arrangements for further advance — the bridge which is 13ft W. B. of Canal was not dry enough. Further report following with scale plan	A.150

Army Form C.2118.

Instructions regarding
War Diaries and Intelligence Summaries
are contained in F.S.Regns, Part II,
and the Staff Manual respectively.
Title pages will be prepared in manuscript.

War Diary
or
INTELLIGENCE SUMMARY

Hour, date, place		Summary of Events and Information	Remarks and references to Appendices
8.1.15 (cont)	7.20p	Message to 23"Co re collecting pumps	A152
	7.40	1 Offr of 537 received - also Offr Cav.B. Opn 321 re arrival of Field Troop. During the afternoon Lt. Mallins, 23rd Co RE went out with a few sprs of London Scottish and blew up a ruined house in front of the line at GIVENCHY.	5.37 Op 321
	11.30p	Signal to Brig. ho 11 received asking for motor lights field troop which had arrived.	Signal to ho 11
	11.35p	Reply sending troop at Oxford 725. U3 During the night Maj. Pritchard Comdg 26 Co was badly wounded whilst directing digging of new trenches E of FESTUBERT.	A 153
9.1.15	8.00	CRE to 1st & 2nd Brigades 8 & 26 Co. Adjutant free from LESEAU re electric pumps Afternoon. See Engineer of Ponts et Chaussees 8 sprs to Fort 8 CRS. + Adjutant to BEUVRY - then to LOZINGHEM to see CRE LAHORE DIVn re electric mains NEUF-ESTUBERT	

Army Form C.2118

Instructions regarding
War Diaries and Intelligence Summaries
are contained in F.S.Regns, Part II,
and the Staff Manual respectively.
Title pages will be prepared in manuscript.

War Diary
or
INTELLIGENCE SUMMARY

Hour, date, place	Summary of Events and Information.	Remarks and references to Appendices
9.1.15 (cont)	GIVENCHY. 2 motor pumps. Back to M.T. Depôt for details. Then to 1st Corps HQ. Des Aff. for authority to purchase two 40 car pumps. Given 5 H.P. petrol engines.	
7p.	Report from Leland Co on floods near GORRE	H 127
7.15.	2nd Ind. Cav. Div. No. 13 Re billets for field troops	2/Ind. Cav Div. No. 13
7.30.	1st Dn GR 4 (SECRET) Re operations	1st Dn GR 4 (SECRET)
8p.	1st Dn S 557, S 555 received	S 557 S 555
	Meant to M. LEGEND arranging for an officer to accompany him to places for purchase of pumps.	correspce attached
10.30	1 Capt S 655 giving approval formally for purchase of pumps if tested & found suitable.	S 655
10.1.15		
8a.	Adjutant 26 C. Hayne with Capts & Lieut of trenches near FESTUBERT. Then to 1st Indian Recce Troop who had worked during previous nt at East S of FESTUBERT. Then to some trenches killed. to 2nd Ind: Field troop who arrived about 2.30 pm. Then trenches centre.	

Army Form C.2118

Instructions regarding
War Diaries and Intelligence Summaries
are contained in F.S.Regns,Part II,
and the Staff Manual respectively. Title pages will be prepared in manuscript.

War Diary
or
INTELLIGENCE SUMMARY

Hour, date, place	Summary of Events and Information.	Remarks and references to Appendices
10.1.15 (cont.)	(1) OC B Coy moves to 23·C·0· & then to trenches S. faced Hazebrouck. Generally improved work during all day. 2 Coys on trenches - not by M.G. replaced a subaltern. The troops had been prepared for a three day artillery bombardment & were accompanied by front of our 2.15 pm — though the M.G. coys' signals up & subsequents held ours to Hangs explicit two sectors 23·C·0· under Lt. BOND & STAFFORD closely followed the assaulting parties between but captured positions in the state of space being judgment relieved by Lt. MAINS' section & two sections in Command & at pockets when stored all day making necessary preparations for assault by in supply furnished it - The whole directed by Capt. MERRING. Messages received and sent during day: 1 Div Sit S, I 591, I 594 GS 281, RE 147 re Letting in our water, Hops RE 171, a note from RE Park A85 Lt. ADAMS, 1st Sqd L.O. visited during day for PARIS with the LEADER of 15th Squadron into trenches	

Army Form C.2118.

Instructions regarding
War Diaries and Intelligence Summaries
are contained in F.S.Regns., Part II,
and the Staff Manual respectively. Title pages will be prepared in manuscript.

War Diary or Intelligence Summary

Hour, date, place	Summary of Events and Information.	Remarks and references to Appendices
1.1.15 8 am	G600 received re pontoons	1st Corps G600
10 "	G503 — do —	G503
10.40	G607 — Special message from G.O.C. 1st Corps previous 24 hrs fighting. Lieut. J. HO RE Owing to fog 2.0 days fighting.	G607
1.20	Adjutant & 2/Lt Jepphis runnen DETH. CAPT. BATTYE, who had previously run an electric welded cable from Stalin to GORE to test insert for insulating electric cable lights in trenches. Together tested the 2 TEST INSERTS Vaseline's insulated electrical himself in DEM'S kill & was preparing plans from fragment & holes prepared fitting so as to run electric pumps.	November 128
2 p	messages from 23rd U. RE Pumps	E.9
6.10 p	messages to C.R.E. 2nd Divn re having new tent labour	E.11
6.40	messages to 26 C.S re purchasing stopps & booms	1st Corps R.E. 157
7 p	messages to 23rd U. re pumps	
	1st Corps R.E. 156 received re bring plant. During last night I Lieut Ireland & Lieut L. CUMBERLAND took an relief party to repelling German trench attack Must hard driven inglistly out of November post our embankment.	

Army Form C.2118.

Instructions regarding
War Diaries and Intelligence Summaries
are contained in F.S. Regns, Part II.
and the Staff Manual respectively. Title pages will be prepared in manuscript.

War Diary
INTELLIGENCE SUMMARY

Hour, date, place	Summary of Events and Information.	Remarks and references to Appendices
11.1.15 (cont:) 7:30 8:30 10:30	1st INDIAN CAV DIV. Reply Msgs replied 2 refces to along 2nd S. of FESTUBERT after going Night. G.622 received G.624 G.626	G.622 G.624 } 1st Ind. G.626 }
	CRE. with Lt Col. MARSHALL CCE 2nd IND CAV DIV to HQ Lucknow Brigade calling at 26 Co. en route. Afterwards to Wfront centre, 2/o Co. 1st Brigade, 9th Field & 19th Coys etc.	
12.1.15 2a	CRE FD8. Co's & with Capt. LEWIS made recon: Town of whole of FESTUBERT line & examined work done by 26 Co. and Indian Field Troops in the evening owing to frm orders that no work be done here the line occupied. The line had to be pulled back & CRE. with Capt LEROY G.S. went to Brigade HQ about 8pm. to decide what should be done. Returned about midnight. During the night a section 26 Co. under 2C WINGATE plus an advanced post about 400ft in front of the line which had been withdrawn on to the actually the new line FESTUBERT - GIVENCHY road. Then reconnoitred about 5 am. During the afternoon the recreation post in rehabilitat:	

Army Form C.2118.

Instructions regarding
War Diaries and Intelligence Summaries
are contained in F.S.Regns.Part II,
and the Staff Manual respectively.
Title pages will be prepared in manuscript.

War Diary
or
INTELLIGENCE SUMMARY

(14)

Hour, date, place	Summary of Events and Information	Remarks and references to Appendices
12.1.15 (cont)	St David lan again evacuated owing to miniwerfer fire — It was occupied by two enemy who were shortly afterwards shelled out by our artillery — 23 v toTauol Cos who had been working continuously till the 1st was evacuated dug & were used to connect west communication head with entanglements.	
11 a	Attack was occupied during night	RS 1.58
5 p	1st Coys Regt re supply of winkles	RS 162
7.30 p	1st Coys Regt 182 re French wire bottle	E 641
10.15	E 641 re munitions	E 644
	E 644 —	
13.1.15	6.30 Report of completion of work re advanced post from 86 Co.	Wyntattalies
	Fa. 1.D. G 647 received	G 647
	9a CRE & Adjutant with Capt. LEROY G.S. to visit 'C' Headquarters (with drains) & then all along Festubert position & see how the line could best be held. Returned to 2nd Trenches & above tried to ascertain by whom & why trench was 2nd shortened. Do' were taken & tests were carried out in his pastry all him action of the line.	

Army Form C.2118.

Instructions regarding
War Diaries and Intelligence Summaries
are contained in F.S.Regns, Part II,
and the Staff Manual respectively. Title pages will be prepared in manuscript.

WAR DIARY or INTELLIGENCE SUMMARY

Hour, date, place		Summary of Events and Information.	Remarks and references to Appendices
13.1.15 (cont.)	4p	Cos. to 23rd & 26th Coys advised.	(15)
	6p	Message from Comdt. Factory re stores available.	R657
	6.30p	S657 advised	
	8.10	Message to 23rd Coy re hurdles	A.169
	8.45	Message to Comd. Factory re disposal of working stores	A.169
	9.30	Reply from 23rd Coy re hurdles.	
	10.30	1st Divl. Order No. 53 received	1st Dn. 53
14.1.15	7am	Message to 26th Coy accompanying to 23 Coy.	A.168
	7.25	C.665 received	F.665
	8.30	Adjutant No Brans. 26th & 23rd & F.Coy James	
	10a	OC. 2nd Dvr. visited CRE & afterwards went over FESTUBERT sector defences with him	
	3.30	Message to 23rd Coy re boring plant.	A.173
	3.45	Message to Adjutant to arrange Corpl. Lindsay & as storekeeper to OC. Nord 3rd Coy.	A.174
	6.45	S.672 from 1st Bns.	S.672
	7pm	S.624 from 1st Bns.	S.624
			1st Corps 165, 171, 172, 175, 175, 172, 172, 172 W. Marshall at RE Park

Army Form C.2118.

Instructions regarding
War Diaries and Intelligence Summaries
are contained in F.S.Regns, Part II,
and the Staff Manual respectively. Title pages will be prepared in manuscript.

War Diary
or
INTELLIGENCE SUMMARY

(16)

Hour, date, place	Summary of Events and Information.	Remarks and references to Appendices
15.1.15/15 7.30	P.667 varied. OBr. started for 2.30 C.O. Adjutant making arrangements for drawing stores from stores. 1 Coy RSW for parade tomorrow. 1 Divr. with invitation to drawing stores from the RE Park. — Arrangements for transport to enable 3 units to obtain the stores. Worked out a conference.	P.667
10.15	Henry to CRE 2nd Div. re pumps	P.175 & 176
11.15	Henry & Empires re identity for stores for RE Park	CE. 216
Noon	Reply from 2nd Div. re pumps	
2/1	Adjutant to HQ Wulverghem to arrange with letter washing accommodation. Then to 26 Coy. — Later to see Genl Rice re greater transport from RE Park	
	CRE. made complete tour of 2nd Divnl Trenches with Capt. Herring — Back to 2nd Brigade HQ. Later was Col. 1st Divison.	
1.45	Henry & 23 Coy re fetching cement from Bailleul	P.172
2.15	Henry & RE Park re same for draws tomorrow. Arrangement made with De Quins Fréres & Bouy.	
7.15	1st Do. & 667 received	P.667

Army Form C. 2118.

Instructions regarding
War Diaries and Intelligence Summaries   W a r   D i a r y
are contained in F.S.Regns,Part II,   or
and the Staff Manual respectively.   INTELLIGENCE SUMMARY
Title pages will be prepared in manuscript.

Hour, date, place	Summary of Events and Information (17)	Remarks and references to Appendices
16.1.15		
7a	Henage & 5th Company re motor pumps	A 160
7.30	£ 655 recieved	£ 659
8.30	Instructions issued by Engineer HQ Stores	A 161
9"	CRE to see Gen. RICE	
	Adjutant to 23rd, 26th, Kns and 85th Div R.E. about	
	2nd Co. to send 2 sections to billet near PONT FIXE	
	for work at GIVENCHY relieving D. trio	
	Also sent one N.C.O. to 1st Bngrs to finish chimneys	
	in bomb thoroughfare.	
	Wrote to 5th Co. R.E. to arrange to handing over 8	
2h	testing auto pumps from PARIS.	
4.00.	CRE to 2nd Brigade, 23rd Co. & No 2 and Co.	£ 655—
5.55	£ 655 recieved	A 162
6.45	Henage & tr. 20 testing pumps	£ 657
7p.	£ 657 recieved	A 163
8p;	Henage & 23 to asking to report a earth augers	£ 695
	£ 695 recieved	
17.1.15		
9a	£ 700 recieved	£ 700
8.55	Henage to GHQ asking to Officers to complete 26 T	A 164
	Lowland Co?	
9"	Adjutant to 5" Co. R.E. 2nd Div. with motor pumps	
	These were handed over & successfully tested	
10a	CRE with Gen. Rice to inspect defences of GIVENCHY	

Army Form C. 2118.

Instructions regarding
War Diaries and Intelligence Summaries
are contained in F.S.Regns, Part II,
and the Staff Manual respectively. Title pages will be prepared in manuscript.

War Diary
or
INTELLIGENCE SUMMARY

(16)

Hour, date, place	Summary of Events and Information	Remarks and references to Appendices
4.1.15 (cont?) 9.30a	Adjutant to 26 CP. Message to Holland re hauling over and labourers to 2nd Div.	A 185
	Message to 23rd Holland CSO putting two sections latter at disposal 1.26 CP. To look at guns cap in steel turning north 20 yds at culvert	A 186 & 187
5.45	£705 received	£705
7p	2 co from 26 CP	£90 242
9p	Message from 2nd Div. re letting over cart labour	PS 242
5.1.15 1.45	Adjutant to Canisen to obtain further detail of work at Overaey. Afterwards repairing shelter "J" Cey". General instructions from CCS.E. front 2 ltr. Sector handed to Maj. Lewis.	E 20
3.45	Message from R.E. Park re pumps available for one 12E 154	12E 154
5.30a	£715 received	£715
7.00a	RE 165 asking re probably requirement of one	RE 165
7a	£705 & £716 ordering parties at Overaey	£705 & £716
8.15?	Message to 26 CP to evacuate all billets	A 150
	North Hazel – now in 2nd Division area	

Army Form C. 2118.

Instructions regarding
War Diaries and Intelligence Summaries
are contained in F.S.Regns, Part II,
and the Staff Manual respectively.
Title pages will be prepared in manuscript.

War Diary or Intelligence Summary

Hour, date, place	Summary of Events and Information	Remarks and references to Appendices
15.1.15 7.20	S.717 received	
7.25	Message to 25th Park re congested man	S.717 A.15
9."	Adjutant 1.26: C.3. then 8.25: C.2 re out retiring A.13. Generally	
12.30	To Capt 8.756 received	
2.1	Notes to 26, 423 C3. to deal w/prisoners	S.756
	r CRS	
5.1	Message from 26 C. re storage accommodation at point F 1x5.	
5.25	To On. J.726 received	J.726
5.40	Message to RS/Nd. re barn wire	A.152
6.45	1st Div. order No 57 received	1st Dn. 57
7.15	Visited by Gen. re G.VENCHY defences	
7."	Message to 25.C. re hospital plates & rewire/brigade	P.156
		A.23.C2
7.40	Message to 2.G.S.A.O. re reinforcements 2.23.C.2	A.155
8.15	R.S.10 in reply to S.751	RS.10
26.1.15 7.20a	S.726 received	S.726
8.40	Cipher Responsing with 2 Lt. Long STRANGEWE	
	K. ring vied Genl. wie active bombard-	
	ment from confirmed	

Army Form C. 2118.

Instructions regarding
War Diaries and Intelligence Summaries
are contained in F.S.Regs.,Part II,
and the Staff Manual respectively.
Title pages will be prepared in manuscript.

War Diary
INTELLIGENCE SUMMARY

Hour, date, place	Summary of Events and Information	Remarks and references to Appendices
20.1.15 (cont'd) 9.00	Adjutant & 2nd Lt. [?] then left for PONT FIXE to see Maj. Lewis. Later met Brig. Gen. Gough, GOC 1st Army Brigade (Givenchy to Givenchy). Afterwards to Rouen & Co. 5th Coy (2nd Mon. Regts.) 2nd Lt. & 2nd Lt. [?] We recalled & sent up to 20th Lt. to be installed. A railway embankment. On support 2 Platoons & detailed to perform and labour in Détourne under the commandant making various arrangements. Latrines &c. Y Hosp in billets.	
	Copy PS 165 22 noon S.40. received	PS 165 S231
	S231 received Order received from 1st Corps that supporting point or strongheart 300 x E of PONT FIXE is to be commenced tomorrow. Obtained 8 N.C.O.'s about this. Arranged to meet OC 2d Gds at 9.15 at PONT FIXE to mark to trace out work on the ground.	
21.1.15	8.45 a.m. Adjutant & PONT FIXE. Met Maj. Lewis RE — Also GOC 3rd W Bge 26 & OC's Munsters & Gloucesters. Work for about 40 rifles on short heads, E. of PONT FIXE reconnoitred and traced.	

Army Form C. 2118.

Instructions regarding War Diaries and Intelligence Summaries are contained in F.S.Regs, Part II, and the Staff Manual respectively. Title pages will be prepared in manuscript.

War Diary or **INTELLIGENCE SUMMARY**

(Erase heading not required.)

Hour, date, place	Summary of Events and Information	Remarks and references to Appendices
21.1.15 (cont)	Visited 23rd Coy & investigated use of potato rake delight.	
5.45p.	G742 received	G742
6p.	Number from G.H.Q. re posting of lieut TOSH to 26th Company.	RE/154/8
	Wire carrying tools & corrugated iron getting from RE Park today & delivered at CAMBRIN. Work started during night on spiral heaps E. of PONT FIXE	
22.1.15		
7.30a	G746 received	G746
9a	Adjutant to PONT FIXE. Visited GIVENCHY keeps & villages defences - & went through WELCH & GLOUCESTER trenches. Afterwards saw work on spiral heaps E. of PONT FIXE — & of 23rd CR	
5p.	Lieut TOSH RE reported on duty with 26th Cy during morning.	
	Handed him 1st & 2nd & distribution of trestle manufactures & similar labour at CORRE	p.8. 153
5.40	1st Bn G752 received	G752
23.1.15		
7.15a	1st Bn G750 received	G750
9a	Adjutant to 23rd CR. Went thro' of 2 complete detail. Organised scheme of defence of W.B.A. later to LaPaus & 26 Companies	
3p	but myr 15 wit went through detailed defence	
6 P.	Scheme of Sector B. received G761 received	G761

Army Form C. 2118.

Instructions regarding
War Diaries and Intelligence Summaries
are contained in F.S. Regns, Part II,
and the Staff Manual respectively.
Title pages will be prepared in manuscript.

War Diary
or
INTELLIGENCE SUMMARY

(22)

Hour, date, place		Summary of Events and Information	Remarks and references to Appendices
24.1.15	7.30 a	1st Div G.769 received	G.769
	9 a	Replied with S.S.O. to POINT FIXE & there is not good 3rd Bgd. It also to see him with a Staff heap.	
		Cinderella shelling by Fah. howitzers of both sides at intervals. This continued all day 12.5- Shells being fired - Damage done & limited later.	
	12.10	Message to 23rd Co. re Scoops for 1st Brigade	A.206
	1 p	Reply	R.B.2
	5.30	12.50 m G.774 received	G.774
	6 p	Memo Off R.E. Park re Stores for Dawn tomorrow	A.209
	6.30	Memo from 1st Corps re "Hastine" available at R.E. Park	R.E.19A
	7.30	Message to 23rd Co. ordering further handles to fence & instruction to Lock gate, at armoury of Bridge Lock keeper at AIRE harried the ready for instant action in case of accident	
	9.30 p	Message to Bomb factory & 23rd Co. reexperimental hand grenades without handles	A.211, A.212
	11.15 p	Reply from 23rd Co. re. re-ordering to current locks & stating it was impossible to do anything with handles	R.B.7
25.1.15	1.30 a	Further report from 23rd Co.	R.B.8
	2 a	Reply from 5th Bgde. re same subject. Forwarded & answer.	G.64 - B.M.27
	2.10	A.213 reply sent	A.213

Army Form C. 2118.

Instructions regarding War Diaries and Intelligence Summaries are contained in F.S. Regns, Part II, and the Staff Manual respectively. Title pages will be prepared in manuscript.

War Diary or Intelligence Summary

(23)

Hour, date, place		Summary of Events and Information	Remarks and references to Appendices
25.1.15 (cont.)	3.30a	Sketch 1 damaged trenches from 23 G.R. by gun rifleing —	Sketch attached
	7.20a	17.Br. 8.775 receved	8.775
		About 7.30am strong attack was made against both sections A.75. Severe fighting continued all day — to Sect 73 local counterattacks restored tranquility of the line with heavy loss to the enemy — In Sect A klld original trenches were not retaken, & a new line formed from during the night through two "Keeps", which had been empty held out all day.	
	9a	Adjutant to le H.Q. Brigade [illegible] BEUVRY	
	4.45p	Brigade to 23: & InFantCo to search dugout which may be required for one Tonight.	P215 - A216
	7p	R.1.55 received — No influenza: a rebuilt after sick	RO.155
	12 midnight	Adjutant to BETHUNE to meet [illegible] and messenger from GHQ re moving dairies in CHURCH Locker — Drive to the Locker	
26.1.15	1am	Called at 23: GR: to [illegible] RSO & Lodr.: Many? launirula? stated that Railway was so blocked that it was impossible to get dairies —	
	2.40a	Gave him 1st Division	S.542
	3.30a	Had to BEUVRY Adjunct & [illegible] to BETHUNE returned to BEUVRY — Crosse? Adjt [illegible] to BEUVRY — Note to 23 & Pr Donn [illegible] GO — 1st Br N.O. & Br Fix	

Instructions regarding
War Dairies and Intelligence Summaries
are contained in F.S.Regns, Part II,
and the Staff manual respectively.
Title pages will be prepared in manuscript

INTELLIGENCE
or
SUMMARY

War Diary

Army Form C. 2118.

Hour, date, place	Summary of Events and Information	Remarks and references to Appendices
26.1.15 (cont'd) 12.10	1st Bn. Operation order no 60 received	Appendix 60
1.30	Returned to BETHUNE	
2/.	Report from OT 76. L/s of enemy's works in front of Section B & description of bomb found at GIVENCHY.	L 78
3.h.	C.R.E. with 9 Off. & 72 guides - conference re several points.	
4.10p	Message to 23rd Co. re party coming bring it from 8th Railway Co. to make sandbag drain in CUINCHY LOCK	A 219, G 565, G 566
6p.	G 565 received	
6.30	G 566 "	
1.15p	Lt. ROMNES with 10 men 6th Railway Co. R.E. arrived by motor bus. Midday R.R. 25 Rs.	A 220, 1st R. 201
10.10p	1st Corps R.R. 201 received	
27.1.15		
6.20a	Lt. ROMNES reported that working party had placed about 3000 filled sandbags in CUINCHY LOCK - also about half completed dam	
7.15	S 97F received	S 97F
9.10	Query to R.E. Park as to what trench pumps are available for trench work - Several having been lost in Sect. A trenches.	
9.30	Query from Bn. to Mairie as to whether another party as required to complete dam tonight.	R 120
4.20	R 223 in reply asking for two parties	A 223

Army Form C. 2118.

Instructions regarding
War Dairies and Intelligence Summaries
are contained in F.S.Regns,Part II,
and the Staff Manual respectively.
Title pages will be prepared in manuscript

War Diary or Intelligence Summary

Hour, date, place	Summary of Events and Information	Remarks and references to Appendices
27.1.15 (cont) 11.Dx	Message from R.E. Park re jumps Copy to 23.Co. by as directed.	3/2
	CRE. stated cont. in the morning not got Pts. S10 Thurs Roussel-Bouin strait boards - references to Breunis current bridges.	
3pm	Message from 1st Bn. that 120 men of 10th Railway Co. are coming for work tonight.	
5.pm	S.965 received	G 965.-
6pm	10. RSLrs party armed Rent straight to CAMBRIN	A 226
7.14pm	A227 & RE Park re stores required tomorrow	A 227
8.15	message to 23rd Co. re sapping for current keeps.	E25-
8.00pm	Reply from 23rd Co.	P5.
10p.	message from 1st Inf. re visit of Anglophenis, Canal Dept	B 920
10.30	message from 3rd Bde. re civilian walking party Stay barred cattle.	Ps 26
28.1.15 3.30 a	Railway Company reported completion of down line Sherm in branch - sow new sapping increased, Patrol, visit of Northern loop closed.	G 95.3 A 228
7.00a	S.950 received	
8.5a	message to 23rd Co. re stores from R.E. Park.	

Army Form C. 2118.

WAR DIARY
or
INTELLIGENCE SUMMARY.
(Erase heading not required.)

Instructions regarding War Diaries and Intelligence Summaries are contained in F.S. Regs., Part II. and the Staff Manual respectively. Title pages will be prepared in manuscript.

(26)

Hour, Date, Place		Summary of Events and Information	Remarks and references to Appendices
28.1.15 (cont)	10 a	Col. NAUDÉ, Chief of War Dept Ports & Crossings with other Officers had a conference during the morning with Gen RICE & CRE about particular road still required in connection with CUINCHY Lock.	
		Reports finally approved on of Railway also were here to find the whereof the Field Companies being continually employed on defensive work.	
	1 p.	R 202 received	R 202
	2 p.	CRE visit 23rd Company	
	2.30	Reported RE: On arrival Officers SEDCOMBE Reported sick	A 231
		Lieut. 26th Company on 23rd knot	
	4 p.	2nd Division R3 received	? P 242 - 13
	4.30		A 232
	6.30 p	Message R.A.H. CARNDUFF to civilian working party for 3 Army H	
	7.30	S 6 received	S 6
		CRE started for ENGLAND on short leave of absence.	
29.1.15	7 am	S 6 received	S 6
	9 a	Adjutant to 2.6 Ireland, & 23rd Companies.	
	1 p.	Report from 3rd Brigade as to Lock of Canal	Nr 1725
		Adjutant to Bomb Factory & Thomas to see ee Backing for Kemmel	A 235
	6.20	S 32 received	S 32
	8 p.	CE 2 from 1st Army	CE 2

WAR DIARY
or
INTELLIGENCE SUMMARY.
(Erase heading not required.)

Army Form C. 2118.

(27)

Hour, Date, Place		Summary of Events and Information	Remarks and references to Appendices
29.1.15 (Cont.)	8.20p	Private declared that MONMOUTHSHIRE Railway Company to send out 7 man to domolition work at CWMCWT LOCK & PONT FIXE. Guard & relief Co. to billet for this Company	A236
	9.20	Reply from Indents? not billet in each dh	A157
	9.30	G.34 received	G34
30.1.15	7a	G.39 received	G29
	8us a	Instrumentation of main Rural Coys - also services re handing out guarding work - also G.S. 1 Coy 22 link a canal.	
	12 units	Detachments arrived at Mal? Clay regulation & Carriage Sou effet Monmouthshire Railway Co.	
		at PONT FIXE Executant billets at BEWLAY.	
	10.30	Reply from 1st Coys 21 being kept	RE24
	1.15p	With detachments at Rails Co. noted Canal Lock, PONT FIXE, Kaust budge East of CWMS	
	5.00p	Report on devices in improvement & not Facilities Bent 15	A235
	6.15p	to Division	A240
	7.45p	Report on being fleet to 1st Coys	G52
	1st By G.50 received		
	9.45p	Report 7.50p on Exp?? Mall? programme tomorrow to include 1 PONT FIXE	P241

Army Form C. 2118.

WAR DIARY
or
INTELLIGENCE SUMMARY.
(Erase heading not required.)

Instructions regarding War Diaries and Intelligence Summaries are contained in F.S. Regs., Part II. and the Staff Manual respectively. Title pages will be prepared in manuscript.

Hour, Date, Place		Summary of Events and Information	Remarks and references to Appendices
31.1.15	7a.m.	G.57 received.	G.57
	11.35p	Report on boring plant forwarded to Adj/Gen 1st 2nd Corps	A 242
		through R. Park STOPBLE providing instruction for use of same.	17243
	3p	O.R.E 2nd Div. arrived to arrange various details in connection with taking over.	
	6.20	G.67 received	G.67
	8.40p	O.R.E 10th Div received. A 244 in reply	A-T-109 — A 244

J.P. Murray. Major. R.E.
m.O.E. 11.8.15

Messages will be found in separate box.

WORK REPORTS

SUMMARY OF WORK PERFORMED BY R.E. UNITS 1st DIVISION.

From MIDDAY ...10th Jan?... to MIDDAY 11th - Jan?

Section.	Company.	Work carried out.
"A"	23rd Co. Lowland C.F.	On 10th: Infantry supported attack on Braenders post & improved parts saved & returned later by instru. and 2 sections Lowland Field Co. on to punch stream but kept on repelling Counter attack & carrying up & fire section making preparations all day 11th for the attack. Same 11th together with dispensary 11th
"B"	Lowland Co. (2 sections)	Preparing Keep at GIVENCHY and drainage, trenches.
"C"	26th C? 1st Ind. Fd Field Troop 7 Field Sec. C.)	Making post for about 200 men in FESTUBERT both days Putting horse along road S of FESTUBERT in state of defence
Miscellaneous	Cpt Wynne for Works Co. 400 civilians	Building up & improving tenements line of defence East of FESTUBERT

Date ...11 - 1 - ...1915.

.... Rank.
W.C.C. R.E.

SUMMARY OF WORK PERFORMED BY R.E. UNITS 1st DIVISION.

From MIDDAY 11/1/15 to MIDDAY 12/1/15

Section.	Company.	Work carried out.
"A"	23 London	Continuous work strengthening lodgement on enemy Embankment - and generally draining, especially on Western Communication Trench
"B"		Nil - material supplied to infantry by 23 C.
"C"	26 Indian Field Troop (attached)	Perimeter of Point d'appui at FESTUBERT nearly completed. Two jumps established. Stated working at infrh SH Church. 50' length of trenchwork on to road at A 6a
Miscellaneous.		2 × 10 hour runs Cap SYMINGTON, Kipland Co continued intermittent two inbound FESTUBERT

Date 12.1.1915.

Capt. Wheeler .... Rank.

Capt R.E. ....

SUMMARY OF WORK PERFORMED BY R.E. UNITS 1st DIVISION.

From MIDDAY 12 Jan......... to MIDDAY 13 –

Section.	Company.	Work carried out.
"A"	23 Durham	Work on Railway Embankment nearly evacuated – Cutting has started from N. communication Railway Drainage
"B"	Lowland	Draining of trenches Wire supplied to trenches essentially N. of canal
"C"	26 – " – 2nd Indian Field Troop (attached)	Road & affair in FESTUBERT. Westwood completed all round – Communications. Clearing preparing commenced – Covered part to Given in road at end figure & Span A 2 completed by night. Marsville 150 × trestwork commenced in Span A 2 c running from road junction S.W. of Le Plantin. To about } completed S. of S.W. Avenue } in proposed trench
Miscellaneous.	–	40 civilians under Capt Symington, Lowland R.E. continued work on intermediate line behind FESTUBERT

13.1. 1915.

J Williams Ra[ ]
[signature] R.E. [ ]

SUMMARY OF WORK PERFORMED BY R.E. UNITS 1st DIVISION.

From MIDDAY .....13ᵗʰ...Jan..... to MIDDAY 14ᵗʰ

Section.	Company.	Work carried out.
"A"	23 {Lowland}	Daiung communication trenches. New emplacement erected in front of machine gun emplacement in gully leading to in front of untenable portion of breast work dugouts.
"B"	{Lowland}	Daiung communication trenches.
"C"	26ᵗʰ 2ⁿᵈ London Fd Troop (attached)	Completed 80/F₂₀ + 1/120 + Breastwork connecting trench 500ˣ N. & E. of Welsh Chapel. One road barricade completed. (Le Plantin road)
Miscellaneous.		Civilians continuing work on intermediate line (nearly completed)

A.J. Wheeler Lt Colonel R.E. Rank.
.....14ᵗʰ........1915.

SUMMARY OF WORK PERFORMED BY R.E. UNITS. 1st DIVISION.

From MIDDAY 14/1th .... to MIDDAY 15th

Section.	Company.	Work carried out.
"A"	23 Infantry	During of communication trenches. Traversing communication trench.
"B"	23 Infantry	During of communication trenches. Improving "Keep".
"C"	26 — 2nd Indian Field Troop	Headcover & loopholes completed in trenches of Hosp Supplies at FESTUBERT which is now capable of being held. Barricade & support road nearing completion + 100' trench completed in reserve between new & old fronts trenches. Completed length of trenches near N.E. LSH CHAPPEL Levelled barricade.
Miscellaneous.	—	Civilian interring & not in intermediate line (neady completed)

Date ....15.1......1915.

J. Mullen Major
..P.R.E..1.Div........ Rank.

SUMMARY OF WORK PERFORMED BY R.E. UNITS 1st DIVISION.

From MIDDAY 15th Jan to MIDDAY 16

Section.	Company.	Work carried out.
"A"	23rd Lowland	Draining communication trenches
"B"	23rd Lowland	Completing GIVENCHY Keep. Draining communication trenches
"C"	26th	Communication & Keep road FESTUBERT point of attack. Restronds along 1st 2nd lines continued. Rear parapet of Tier is being taken over by 5th Company R.E. 2nd Division
Miscellaneous.		Civilians continuing returned at time. No. II completed known 7 later handed over X 2-Ba.

Date 16. 1. 1915.

C. A. Wheatley .... Rank.
Mr. 1st 1915.

SUMMARY OF WORK PERFORMED BY R.E. UNITS 1st DIVISION.

From MIDDAY 16 Jan......... to MIDDAY 17/1/15

Section.	Company.	Work carried out.
"A"	23 (Field)	Draining trenches
"B"	23 (Field)	Draining trenches (The ration & supply trenches b 26 (e.)
"C"	26th Nahasos b 5th L.I. 2nd Division	Medical Cover, Loopholes, & communications FESTUBERT Pont d'Achin. Afas in breastwork n LE PLANTIN line completed
Miscellaneous.		1 N.C.O. provided as interpreter btw: Indians Hdts & Indian Div b 2nd Div: tomorrow.

Date 17.1..........1915.

J. Muldoon Major. Rank.
for C.R.E. 1 Div.

SUMMARY OF WORK PERFORMED BY R.E. UNITS 1st DIVISION.

From MIDDAY 17th Jan. to MIDDAY 18th.

Section.	Company.	Work carried out.
"A"	23rd Co. ½ Lowland Co.	Pumping & clearing trenches. Improvement of Keep.
"B"	26 Co. ½ Lowland Co.	Improving & making foot bridges over Canal. Draining & clearing communication trenches.
"C"	Taken on by 2nd Division	
Miscellaneous.		Civit labourers handed over to C.R.E. 2nd Divn.

18 . 1 . 1915.

R. Hutchison
Capt.
R.E. C.R.E. 1st Divn.

SUMMARY OF WORK PERFORMED BY R.E. UNITS 1st DIVISION.

From MIDDAY 16 Jan to MIDDAY 15

Section.	Company.	Work carried out.
"A"	23rd London	Improvement & Keep cleaning up old communication trenches. Pumping water dug outs & tracks saw.
"B"	26th London	taking round Givenchy Pont d'affair repairing horses lines, road to defence. Pumping & clearing communication trenches.
"C"		
Miscellaneous.		

Date 15. 1. 1915.

J.A. ..... Major Rank.
R.E. 1st Div.

SUMMARY OF WORK PERFORMED BY R.E. UNITS 7t DIVISION.

From MIDDAY ...15 Jan...... to MIDDAY 20 —

Section.	Company.	Work carried out.
"A"	23" Coy R.E.	Darning justing down flooring in hect+communication trench Interviews of trench earthwork Repairing & draining later communication trench
"B"	26 Coy R.E.	Working round keep & making new dug out in keep Repairing horses lines, road to out of defence Pushed & clearing communication trench S.P. B1
"C"		
Miscellaneous		

Date ...20/1/......1915.

.... Rank.
....

SUMMARY OF WORK PERFORMED BY R.E. UNITS 1st DIVISION.

From MIDDAY ...20..Jan..... to MIDDAY 21st.

Section.	Company.	Work carried out.
"A"	23 Lowland	Improvement of keep continued. Improvement of keep communication about 100 front EGYP hnine gallery commenced from trickstell to N Salient. commenced from trickstell to N Salient. I Princetino
"B"	26 Lowland	Improvement of "Twenty Cup Keep" & defence of horses continued. 20' x breast-worky slot & hind out in front of throwing head to breast supplement extends to NAMUR to Lt LongGATE improvement & clearing octoval communication headlong?
"C"	B	Supporting work parties 40 rifles or that heap 50' x E of PONT FIXE breezy during the evening. will be continued 5 past. 26 lot tonight
Miscellaneous.		

Date ....21...1...1915.

.... Rank.
Jr C.R.E. 1921.

SUMMARY OF WORK PERFORMED BY R.E. UNITS ●t DIVISION.

From MIDDAY ...21.1.14... to MIDDAY 22

Section.	Company.	Work carried out.
"A"	23rd Kholand	Work on "Keep" completed. Dawning improving breastworks communication Road, where has also been wiring left of front of old Kent Road. River Gallery continued
"B"	26	Improvement of stores — making niches for profiles — commencement of wooden bomb proof shelter in "Keep" R.Edmencer. Continuing to making mines across road. Connecting work at 2nd artillery trench commenced — the trenches was completed last to hundred tonight + wiring completed as communication trenches
"C"	K Holand	Continuing other communication to council K front to trenches.
Miscellaneous	NOTE	Wiring between TRENCH FARM MAMETZ reported yesterday should read "starting from road near lookout + running South"

Date ....22.1..1915.

.......J.N.Wilson..Major.... Rank.
.......R.E.E. gonn...........

SUMMARY OF WORK PERFORMED BY R.E. UNITS 8t DIVISION.

From MIDDAY ...22.1.15... to MIDDAY 23'

Section.	Company.	Work carried out.
"A"	23 Colonel	Driving, repairing W. Comm? Trench & making E of OLD KENT ROAD Trenches E & W Comm? Trenches. Mine firm included extended. Barb Defense laid across main road from ex front pt. the tunnel
"B"	96 Colonel	GUNNERS KEEP - H.Q dug out made & second emplacement machine Gun - the Keep is now complete. Loopholes in houses behind just opposite completed. Wire support to put in front Keep - fire trenches completed - Comm? S. nearly 30 x 60 inundated completed in part. Contained about 60 x wire Ditch in part of GLOUCESTERS. Contained work & defence of house at S.W. corner of orchard between N.B. Communit Rock.
"C"	}	
Miscellaneous	Colonel	Contained drawing & clearing orchard comm't trench

Date ....25.1....1915.

J. K..........
Lieut.
...................Lt Col R.E.

SUMMARY OF WORK PERFORMED BY R.E. UNITS 1st DIVISION.

From MIDDAY 2 3 Jan to MIDDAY 24

Section.	Company.	Work carried out.
"A"	23 Co? Rnd	Work on Trenches & post & convert trench & OLD KENT ROAD. Mine gallery at W12 subsequent continued No 1 & 2 day. Gun platform to incorporate gun made in "Keep". Listening Mine near END of OLD KENT ROAD cleared & drained.
"B"	26 Co? Rnd	New post & gun emplacements West wall completed — but a good deal of revetment & clearing will be required when ground is available. Digging of firing at corner of Orchard continued. Overhead communication at the rear of wall continued. Clearing & communication trench along road of short loops on West.
"C"		Wiring in front of GLOUCESTERS continued.

Miscellaneous.

Date 24.1. 1915.

J. Richardson
Major Rank.
for CRE 1 Div?

SUMMARY OF WORK PERFORMED BY R.E. UNITS 1st DIVISION.

From MIDDAY ...25. Jan... to MIDDAY ...26...

Section	Company	Work carried out.
"A"	23rd ½ Coy/Pard	Work as for 25-26. Continued till stopped by all clear morning of 25. During night 25-26. Men had 120yds long made in front of existing communication trench running from Keep to La Bassée Road. Holes in wall near ANNEQUIN repaired. Party fixed to Brewery Sluice in crumpholes but failed owing to hostile shells.
"B"	26th ½ Coy/Pard	Work by day continued as for 25-26. By night 250x revel and delate places from French Front N.W. 2/00x To Sz. Wire secured about three quarters of from at corner of orchard N.J Brewery Lock. Wire apparent front of Lenox trench covered up by Lt. Wingate.
"C"		Good deal of communication trenches in B, improved & repaired
Miscellaneous.		

Date ...26 - 1...1915.

.......Johnson........
..............Major.............Rank.
............C.R.E. 1st Division...........

SUMMARY OF WORK PERFORMED BY R.E. UNITS 1st DIVISION.

From MIDDAY 26- Jan. to MIDDAY 27"

Section.	Company.	Work carried out.
"A"	23" ½ Coy Rwd	Digging salt infantry parties new second line of communications from the keep in S.E. direction to main road near ruined tower. Wire & keep advanced & strengthened generally. New keep near convent church commenced
"B"	26" ½ Coy Rwd	No report received - Work as yesterday. Wire road to be reported on
"C"		
Miscellaneous.		

Date 27..1..1915.

J.P. Williams
Lt. .... Rank.
for O.C. 1/1st Coy.

SUMMARY OF WORK PERFORMED BY R.E. UNITS 1st DIVISION.

From MIDDAY 1st 26th Jan to MIDDAY 27th
                                          27th
                                          28.

Section.	Company.	Work carried out.
"A"	23rd ½ Lowland	Assisted in making new trench on right flank up to LA BASSEE road. — Completed communication trench leading to Cuinchy from right flank. Continued front of culvert which was concrete cluved and communicated head from culvert to west.
"B"	26th ½ Lowland	Wiring continued in front of trenches in B3 & B2. Loop hole form N of lock continued. Driving communication trades completed. Head of dugout and concrete house floor up by Lt WINGATE.
"C"		
Miscellaneous		

Date 28. 1. 1915.

.... Signature
Major........... Rank.
R.E. ½ Lowland Div.

SUMMARY OF WORK PERFORMED BY R.E. UNITS 1st DIVISION.

From MIDDAY 26th Jan to MIDDAY 29th.

Section.	Company.	Work carried out.
"A"	23rd R.M.land	New supporting trench - CUINCHY - Established talks at NW corner - to Sugfact protected towards NW. Traverses & wire all improved for 300m. Trenches from 100" S of CUINCHY cemetery - new trench at E end of orchard behind farm & orchard from horse lines.
"B"	"	CUINCHY Keep - Sapped trench along S side about 2nd from face - started saps in several places from both N & S faces. Wire are being continued without break.
"C"	26th R.M.land	151 - Walthamtown trench work probably done repairing parapet - nearly finished - S. communication trench good as far as to edge of short bank. Completed drainage of farm across hollow to half of lock. Cleared about 250 ft of ditch along S side & need to improve feed of farm from S side of spinney across front of squad.
Miscellaneous		B3 horsing, with Head gues 202th completed except the section.

Date 29=1= 1915.

J. A. Waller Major R.E. Rank.
for C.R.E. 1st Division

SUMMARY OF WORK PERFORMED BY R.E. UNITS 1st DIVISION.

From MIDDAY 29th Jan to MIDDAY 30th /15

Section.	Company.	Work carried out.
"A"	23rd ½ Norland	Saps continued at A & B (see attached rough sketch) progress about 8 yds. Sap started at C to connect for head to company on left.
"B"	26 ½ Ireland	2nd line position dug from CUINCHY CHURCH for about 400 yds South along East ½ road
"B"	½ Ireland	Both comm. trenches in B1 continued. Wire obstacle was prepared & 4 or 5 rows ready to put down at in front of big dike – but the light was never [illegible] [illegible] of impossible to get in front of the dike at all.
Miscellaneous.		

Date 30=1= 1915.

Signature — Major R.E. Rank.
For C.R.E. 1st Division.

SUMMARY OF WORK PERFORMED BY R.E. UNITS 1st DIVISION.

From MIDDAY 30 Jan to MIDDAY 31/2

Section.	Company.	Work carried out.
"A"	23rd	Sap at B.D.& E advanced about 5 yds each & head B traverses with sandbags. Sap A advanced 2 yds. Army & trestles in sort. Sap C & trestles advanced about 25 yds. Through huts. Made a rough embrasure & loophole of sandbags in steel.
"B"	Matter ??	The two Sap enclosures completed except at A. Traverse DC & new T/rey head. Sap made to top Newbehavior. Comm. trench started in hills, E new 2 ft 6. New 6,000 trench bay 6000 Eng. starting.
"C"	26 "Labord"	Communication trenches continued in B1. & section B2 & B3 nearly completed along about 900 ft front. Dug. Read un shelter.
Miscellaneous.	Ammunition Newton ?? (into the temp?)	Completed ??? to sandbag dam in South channel of ??? this no her shot & 1000 filled bags in three dams. 1 winch lock. Prepared bags for ??? ??? point F125.

Date 31.1. 1915.

V Murayon ??? Rank.
Jps C.R. ???

SUMMARY OF WORK PERFORMED BY R.E. UNITS 1st DIVISION.

From MIDDAY 31º Jan...... to MIDDAY 2ª Feb.

Section.	Company.	Work carried out.
"A"	23rd Coy. ½ Island Coy. 5 x 226 - 2nd Division	Commenced a TRANSEE ROAD - 50 yds of wiring & cwwire - Completed all round supporting point near Cuinchy Church - made all round 3 points d'appui at cross roads S. of Port Fixe and provision stationers - rates noted in then orders -
"B"	26th Coy. ½ Inland	Strengthened Keep noted M. 732 - About 290 yds new entanglements put in front of Keep & 131.
"C"		
Miscellaneous.	Fransporting Material (Petites etc)	Commenced bringing under PONT F-1XE - 6 large piles sunk & sandbag barricades will probably be finished tonight.

Date 1st February 1915.

J. Hudson .... Capt R.E. Rank.
for C.R.E. 1st Division

WAR DIARY

C.R.E. 1st DIVISION

February

1915

Army Form C. 2118.

WAR DIARY
OR
INTELLIGENCE SUMMARY. /R. 1ST DIVISIONAL ENGINEERS

No 7   February 1915

(Erase heading not required.)

Instructions regarding War Diaries and Intelligence Summaries are contained in F.S. Regs., Part II and the Staff Manual respectively. Title pages will be prepared in manuscript.

Hour, Date, Place	Summary of Events and Information	Remarks and references to Appendices
BETHUNE		
1.2.15 4.20 a.m.	Lt. THOMAS reported six barges successfully sunk at PONT FIXE	R.E. 217
10.30	Message from 1st Corps re stoves available in R.E. Park	
2.15 p.m.	Adjutant to PONT FIXE re bridge-head defences; back to BEUVRY to arrange to-night work on barrage.	
4 p.m.	G. 94 received. This refers to the successful retaking of certain posts & French just S. of Canal by 4th Bde. (Temporarily under orders of 1st Dn)	G. 94
4.30 p.m.	R.B.3 received - re relief by 11th Co.	R.B.3
6.5	G. 98	G. 98
7.30	G. 100 & Tactical Report	G. 100 & Tactical Report Message appended.
12 mn.	Monmouthshire Co. report PONT FIXE barrage completed.	
2.2.15		
7.30 a.m.		
10 a.m.	Adjutant to 23rd Co. & PONT FIXE to see bridge-head defences & barrage - also to howland Co. re repairs to LEPREOL - ANNEQUIN RD.	G. 103
12 noon	Report from howland Co. on road	A 522
2 p.m.		A 162
3	Adjutant visited Pont et Chavasses office re civilian working parties for this road	
	Report from O.C. R.3rd Co. on various types of pump	R.B. 1

(73989) W4141—463. 400,000. 9/14. H.&J.Ltd. Forms/C. 2118/10.

Army Form C. 2118.

WAR DIARY
or
INTELLIGENCE SUMMARY.
(Erase heading not required.)

Instructions regarding War Diaries and Intelligence Summaries are contained in F.S. Regs., Part II. and the Staff Manual respectively. Title pages will be prepared in manuscript.

Hour, Date, Place	Summary of Events and Information	Remarks and references to Appendices
BETHUNE.	(2)	
2.2.15. (contd) 4 pm.	C.R.E. 2nd Div'n again came to settle further details of handing over E. Anglian F.d. Co. R.E. (T) from 26 Co. – 11th Co. from 23rd Co.	386 and 401
7.40	Message from R.E. Park re plain wire and hyposcopes	G 1115
9.0.	Message re sand bags for 4th Bde.	G A 13.
9.5	Message re relief of 23rd Co.	Message appended.
10.30	Lorry sent to bank factory for 1000 sand bags for 23rd Co.	"
3.2.15		
7.45 a.m.		G 120
9.30	Lorry sent to R.E. Park for sand-bags	A1
9.45	3rd Bde asks for 5000 sand-bags.	# 9 13 E
	Message rec'd that bottled wine is urgently required for bridge – head post at PONT FIXE – Arranged with C.R.E. 2nd Div'n that this should be obtained from 2nd Div. Amm. Col., a sent straight up.	
2.30.	Message from 1st corps that two Fd. Co.s will be left at disposal of 2nd Div'n.	G 18.
2.35	Message re attachment of Major Addison to 1st Corps	G 19.

Army Form C. 2118.

WAR DIARY
or
INTELLIGENCE SUMMARY.
(Erase heading not required.)

Instructions regarding War Diaries and Intelligence Summaries are contained in F.S. Regs., Part II. and the Staff Manual respectively. Title pages will be prepared in manuscript.

(3)

Hour, Date, Place		Summary of Events and Information	Remarks and references to Appendices
BETHUNE			
3.2.15.	6.30 p.m.	1st Division Order No. 61 received	G 141 Order appended.
	8.21		
	6.0 p.m.	G.O.C. 1st Div. issued verbal instruction to Major Russell Brown to join him to-morrow as 2/C.R.E. during Lt. Col. Schreiber's absence on leave	
4.2.15		Major Addison left for 1st Corps after handing over to Major Russell - Brown.	
		Baggage & personnel of 1st D.E. left BETHUNE & proceeded	A.R.B.L
	3 p.m.	to MARLES, arriving there at 3 p.m.	
	6 p.m.	CRE reported to Div 2 HQ that 26th Co. had been at more or less continuous work since Xmas and asked that it should be withdrawn as soon as possible.	
5-2-15	MARLES	Lt Parkes, although slightly wounded & requiring X ray treatment, was allowed to proceed on ordinary leave to 17th inst.	C3, C4, h 2 et, F67
		Capt. J.H. Richard joined 26th Fd. Co.	

Army Form C. 2118.

WAR DIARY
or
INTELLIGENCE SUMMARY.
(Erase heading not required.)

Hour, Date, Place	Summary of Events and Information	Remarks and references to Appendices
MARLES		
6-1-15	Messages regarding cable or wire rope for stretching across canal.	RB 4, RB 8
	C.R.E. issues instructions regarding discipline of Horse proceeding on leave	RB 3
	Memo from 1st Corps expresses Commander-in-Chief's appreciation of the good work done by the troops during past six weeks	G 432
	Lieut Mullins, 23rd Co. & 2/Lt Rice, 26th Co. granted 8 days leave.	
7-1-15	26th Fd. Co. left 2nd Divn and rejoined 1st D.E.; marching to new billets at LAPUGNOY in 3rd Bde Area. Capt. Richard proceeded at PONT FIXE to assist E. Anglian Fd. Co.	C 7
	2nd Lieuts J. Wilson and J.S. Inglis joined howitzer Fd. Co.	R.E. 670
3.30 pm	A/C.R.E. visited S.O. to C.E. at ST OMER re R.E. stores, reports on pumps, boring gear, bombs, etc	A 8
8.30 pm	Lt. Col. Schreiber returned from leave & resumed duties of C.R.E.	
8-1-15		
9.30 am.	C.R.E. reported to 1st Divn & subsequently proceeded to AIRE to see C.E. 1st Army	

Army Form C. 2118.

WAR DIARY
or
INTELLIGENCE SUMMARY.
(Erase heading not required.)

Instructions regarding War Diaries and Intelligence Summaries are contained in F.S.Regs., Part II. and the Staff Manual respectively. Title pages will be prepared in manuscript.

(5)

Hour, Date, Place	Summary of Events and Information	Remarks and references to Appendices
MARLES		
8-2-15.	CRE & Adjutant visited 2nd F.E. Co. & subsequently attended lecture by G.O.C. 1st Division at 2nd Bde. Hd. Qrs. ALLOUAGNE.	G39, A26, RB2
9-2-15.	Lieut. Parker proceeded on leave. CRE visited 23rd Co. in billets at HURIONVILLE. Arrangements were made with Division for 1st D.E. co-operation in Training of Infantry. [Which in reverse of lists of R.E. stores required from R.E. Park and Bomb Factory were prepared.]	RE/541/3, 534, A 637 C12, RB5, RB 8, RB9, RB 2
10-2-15.	A 1½ Ton lorry was sent to R.E. Park to fetch stores required for Training Infantry. CRE visited 2nd D.E. & arranged that Colonel Fd. Co. should remain with 2nd Division until 20th inst. Arranged that 26th Fd. Co. should work with 2nd & 3rd Bdes. for Training purposes. Lieut. Calthrop joined 26th Co. CRE sent to 1st Div. a memo. regarding training in use of hand-grenade. Transport was sent to R.E. Park and Bomb Factory for further supply of stores for use in training Infantry.	R.E 746, G 75, RB 7, RB 2, RB 5, RB 10, Copy appended.
11-2-15.	CRE issued special instructions regarding to wiring of Infantry in Trench-work, hut-housing, etc.	J 16, R-B, H.Q.R.E. 1st Div. N°95 (G) & appendices

Army Form C. 2118.

WAR DIARY
or
INTELLIGENCE SUMMARY.
(Erase heading not required.)

Instructions regarding War Diaries and Intelligence Summaries are contained in F.S. Regs., Part II. and the Staff Manual respectively. Title pages will be prepared in manuscript.

Hour, Date, Place	Summary of Events and Information	Remarks and references to Appendices
MARLES 11-2-15. (contd.)	Letter issued by 1st Division complimenting R.E. of 1st Division on good work done by them during past six weeks.	Copy attached.
12-2-15	C.R.E. visited 1st Corps and proceeded subsequently to ST OMER. Capt. Richard rejoined, reporting personally at 1st D.E. at 3 p.m; proceeded to take over from Major Russell Brown the duties of Adjutant. 2nd D.E. reported that an Officer should be sent to explain the arrangement of mines around GIVENCHY KEEP	W 34 RB 2, RB 7,
13-2-15	C.R.E. proceeded to CHOCQUES & discussed proposals for forming a body of trained miners. 2/Lr. Tosh proceeded to GIVENCHY. C.R.E. visited 26th F.C. in afternoon & discussed various points in connection with its training in Mily. Engineering. Major Russell Brown resumed command of 23rd Fd. Co. R.E.	RB 3 608, 1st Div. No 957 T 1, RB 3 1,
14-2-15	C.R.E. visited 2nd Bde. Head quarters & discussed training of Infantry.	M 825, 619, 142, JR 4, JHR 2, JR 5,
15-2-15	C.R.E. inspected 26th Fd. Co. in marching order. General Haking delivered a lecture on the training of the Division; Officers & Senior NCO's of R.E. Co. attended - also CRE & a/adj.	Parade state appended TR 13 TR 14 - TR 12, & Key

WAR DIARY
or
INTELLIGENCE SUMMARY.
(Erase heading not required.)

Army Form C. 2118.

Hour, Date, Place	Summary of Events and Information	Remarks and references to Appendices
MARLES 16-2-15.	A memorandum regarding the formation, organization and letter development of means for conducting mine warfare, issued by 1st Army, & handed in by 1st Corps, was received from 1st Div. together with memo marked (A) and (B) on same subject. CRE visited 3rd Bde. Capt. HERRING was accidentally wounded whilst superintending instruction of Infantry in hand-bomb throwing. 23rd Fd. Co. moved this afternoon into new billets at RAIMBERT.	1st Army No. G.S. 42. P.S. 1, Q 672, Q 683, H.G. 10 ¶ Report attached.
17-2-15	CRE to LILLERS and saw Capt. Herring in No 4 Clearing H. A court of Enquiry assembled & reported upon the accident. Capt. Herring was sent down to BOULOGNE. CRE visited 1st Corps. 8.3-15 Perry went to ST RAZEELE to attain further supply of stores. Capt. Forsyth RAMC proceeded on 6 days leave	Copy of Proceedings & of CRE's report thereon are appended. OR 1, OR 2, OR 1, TR 3. Report in killed Tapes C/18 G. 145

017# WAR DIARY
INTELLIGENCE SUMMARY.
(Erase heading not required.)

Army Form C. 2118.

(8)

Hour, Date, Place	Summary of Events and Information	Remarks and references to Appendices
DIMPLES 18-2-15	C.R.E. to 26th Co. & had experiment made with a view to discovering its cause of its accident on Tuesday. Copy of his report is attached. In accordance with orders from 1st Corps the C.R.E. nominated 23rd Fd. Co. R.E. to relieve 1st Lowland Fd Co R.E. on 22nd inst. 2nd D.E. asked that the question of relieving the Lowlands by another Fd. Co. from 1st Div'n might be allowed to stand over for a few days, & was eventually agreed by 1st Corps that the matter should be settled by mutual arrangement between the C.R.E's of 1st & 2nd Divisions.	JR 9 A 500 JR 7 R53 REZI W1 C/21 Q707 E 38 Q720 (X) (Y) 5744 C/20 R 939 Q 731 Q 752
19-2-15 (Friday)	C.R.E. visited 2nd D.E. & subsequently witnessed at BETHUNE a demonstration of a new petrol bomb. 2nd Lieut. H.F. Seabrook left 26th Co under orders for 56th Co. 3rd Division. An accident occurred this afternoon in 26th Co. billet whilst fuze, detonators, etc were being fitted to hand bombs, two sappers severely wounded - several others slightly. Memo from O/c R.E. Base Records re promotions in the field.	E40 C/21 RE 22 JR11 W1 JR 12 JR 13 Q 751 Q 754 Q 752 JR 14 JR 15 Q 753 Q 745 attached
20-2-15	A court of Enquiry assembled at 26th Co. billet to investigate yesterday's accident. Copy of proceedings and of CRE's remarks attached. CRE 2nd Div'n expressed his appreciation of work done by 1st Lowland F.C.G. Major hems returned from leave at 10.45 am, having been delayed JR 20 from Folkestone being delayed by Admiralty.	ca 4 Copy attached Q 772 JR 18 Q 775 H.Q.R.E.

Army Form C. 2118.

WAR DIARY
or
INTELLIGENCE SUMMARY.

(Erase heading not required.)

Instructions regarding War Diaries and Intelligence Summaries are contained in F.S. Regs., Part II. and the Staff Manual respectively. Title pages will be prepared in manuscript.

Hour, Date, Place	Summary of Events and Information	Remarks and references to Appendices
MARLES 21-2-15 (Sunday)	Capt. Bell returned from leave at 2 a.m. A report on inaccuracies in measuring tapes was sent to 1st Div. Copy of report is marked (Z) and attached	A 203 5 39 Q 210 R.E. 24 758 (x) 210 (Y) T 24 c/26 SR 23
22-2-15	C.R.E. & Adj. to 23rd Co. for inspection of the company in marching order. 2/Lt. Rose took over duties of 4/6ths & Capt. Richard proceeded on leave. Captain E.F.S. Dawson reported for duty with 23rd Fd. Co. R.E. The Brigadier General Cmndg. 1st Division directs the Court of Inquiry to reassemble at Ref. to record sufficient evidence to give a firm indication as to the reason for the opinion that Sinr (1st Div. N° 1030) be given after Lt. March. 1st Div. N° 1041 notifies that no leave will (inaudible) be given after 1st March.	1st Div. N° 1039, 43 Ca 1, 24, R2

Army Form C. 2118.

WAR DIARY
or
INTELLIGENCE SUMMARY.
(Erase heading not required.)

Hour, Date, Place	Summary of Events and Information	Remarks and references to Appendices
MARLES 23.2.15	(10) Court of Enquiry on Bank Explosion re-assembled at 26th Co. Lorry sent to RE Park for mining stores. CRE and adj. to 1st Hunstand Fd. Co. RE — inspection at 3 pm Capt. Dawson granted 5 days leave. Message (copy attached - G 192) received ordering 26th Co to proceed with 3rd Bde in relief of 5th Co (1st 5th Bde) in FESTUBERT section. 1st Div No 134 (G) — 1st 100 N.C.o, & men tested by 26th Co in mining will tomorrow be attached, half to 23rd & half to 26th Co. Any officer will be temporarily attached with each party & will be replaced ultimately by specially appointed officers. War Office letter No 150/General No 2739 (M.S.1), dated 16th inst. regarding promotion of Regimental officers in succession to those reported to be Prisoners of war in mining received.	A.5, RE 27, R.7, M 276, DAGW 132 w 687 { G 192

WAR DIARY or INTELLIGENCE SUMMARY

Army Form C. 2118.

Hour, Date, Place	Summary of Events and Information	Remarks and references to Appendices
MARLES 24-2-15	Major Arthur, Lieuts Shanks & Clarke, 1st Rundard Fd. Co. granted 8 days leave. Notification received that 2/Lieut Wingate 2/5 Co. has been awarded D.S.O.	RE 249 B1 RE 71 W1
2.30 p.m.	CRE to 26th Co. & thence to CRE 2nd Divn to arrange about WEG for 26th Co. Finally settled that its should take over GORRE Brewery from 5th Co.	
25-2-15 9.15 a.m.	CRE inspect 1st Signal Co. in marching order. CRE visited 23rd Co.	B7 RB1 RS 3 Cr 20
3 p.m.	Order received re movement of 23rd Co. with 1st Bde on 29th. 1st Divl No 115(S) directs that RE Artillery will cease to reorganise for fighting Trench Mortars & that an officer in each Bde will be placed in charge of them. 1st Div. No 151 (G) — instructions regarding Signal Service with a Division. Lieut. PARKES admitted to hospital.	x7 L10 G.914 SE143 R5 G 207 RE 85 4-9.M.E

Army Form C. 2118.

WAR DIARY
or
INTELLIGENCE SUMMARY.
(Erase heading not required.)

Instructions regarding War Diaries and Intelligence Summaries are contained in F.S. Regs., Part II and the Staff Manual respectively. Title pages will be prepared in manuscript.

Hour, Date, Place		Summary of Events and Information	Remarks and references to Appendices
MARLES		(12)	
26-2-15	9.45 a.m.	Huns proceed to R.E. Park & returns with 100 periscopes.	R1 RB1 R2
	2 p.m.	C.R.E. proceeds with G.O.C. 1st Bde to LATOURET, returning	RB2 R3 R6
	6.30 p.m.	c/adj. to HINGES re new billets.	
		1st Division Order No 62 (copy attached) orders a move to HINGES.	1st Division No 62
		G.H.Q. directs that head. P.MRNES casually should be made good from 26th Co. which has 5 battalions.	R.E./616
		Memo. from S.W.O. G.H.Q. explains use of Capo Commercial Octuple 5 states that Blackline & Gunmetal (Suitable for use with Ultra copies) will be kept in R.E. Park.	R.E. 30
29-2-15	7.30 a.m.	Capt Forsyth R.A.M.C. returns from leave.	
	9.30 a.m.	Men of 1st Sig. Co. remanded for F.G.C.M.	a 1600 Re
	11 a.m.	F.G.C.M. sits on Spr Quinlan 1st Sig. Co.	R7
	2 p.m.	C.R.E. with G.S.O.3 c/adj. to HINGES to new Divisional area.	H. 4. R.E.

Army Form C. 2118.

WAR DIARY
or
INTELLIGENCE SUMMARY.
(Erase heading not required.)

Instructions regarding War Diaries and Intelligence Summaries are contained in F.S. Regs., Part II. and the Staff Manual respectively. Title pages will be prepared in manuscript.

(13)

Hour, Date, Place	Summary of Events and Information	Remarks and references to Appendices
MARLES		
28.2.15		
9.30 a.m.	Div¹ Eng² HQ. move to HINGES, arriving 12 noon.	G.220 Q.750
2.30 p.m.	CRE. visits Brick Factory re sand bags. Arrangements made for 20,000 from 2nd Division & 2 lorries to go to STRAZEELE	904 Progress Report.

[signature] RE.
Capt. for
CRE 1st Div¹

Work Reports

Training Scheme

SUMMARY OF WORK PERFORMED BY R.E. UNITS 1st DIVISION.

From MIDDAY 1st Feb. to MIDDAY 2nd Feb.

Section	Company	Work carried out
"A"	23rd	Previous night's work on BASSÉE Road in engine completed by wiring French Trench for firestanding. 477 men walm-filled & wired to N. Fence, keep 2 line. Into a wiredportion (see attached sketch) in of Road. Sandbag tresiade formed at 79F & North facing S. Position with sandbags. Sandbag lining on emplacement West of B. Traverses made at C. D.E.F.
"B"	½ Kent Land	Red line carried two new lines of fire on sides to front J B and A 2nd line trench dug. up S wire vehemented & road by keep truck west at G. Wiring 2nd round wires 2 and S. North of POINT FIXE.
"C"	2/6 ½ Ko Land	Communicate Trench continued in B1 — There is still much water in S Trench & position very slow. About 190 yds of new entanglement put in front of left of B1. About 200 yds wiring in front of B2 Kighler old wire saturated & destroyed. Water level ——————— Completed farmary under POINT FIXE.
Miscellaneous	2nd Anst # 1/4 O.R.E.	2500m E English PICKE transversely Queens. Completed M.700 of bridge head rail — 3 of wiring all inboard.

Date 2nd Feb. 1915.

J. W. Walker Major R.E.
for C.R.E. 1st Divn.
.... Rank.

SUMMARY OF WORK PERFORMED BY R.E. UNITS 1st DIVISION.

From MIDDAY 2nd Feb. to MIDDAY 3rd Feb.

Section.	Company.	Work carried out.
"A"	23rd Monmouth R.E. (att 2) ½ LoramdCo	4 trup nets sold, p 4 men made in CULVERT post - 3 blue heads dug from junction of CUINCHY – LA BASSÉE road to East of trenches near PONT FIXE
"B"	26th ½ S. Anglian & Nº 3 4 (working parties)	booing in front of trenches – the whole front B Shrs. be finished tonight – Continuing trolly line past at Distillery –
"C"		/
Miscellaneous.		/

Date ... 3rd Feb. ...1915.

J. Mauriwi Major R.E. Rank.
for C.R.E. 1st Div.

SUMMARY OF WORK PERFORMED BY R.E. UNITS 1st DIVISION.

From MIDDAY 28th Feb. 1915 to MIDDAY 1st March

Section.	Company.	Work carried out.
3rd Bde. "A" FESTUBERT	26th	1. Improved 20ˣ of old breastwork 2. Constructed 85ˣ " new " 4. Revetment for 45ˣ erected infantry to fill in 5. Work continued at Point "M" — Work now nearly completed.
1st Bde. "B" RUE DuBOIS	23rd.	① Reconnaissance of new section by Company Officers ② Collection of material for work.
"C"		Note. 1st Lowland F.E. Co. has not yet commenced work.
Miscellaneous.		

Date 1st March 1915.

ElsRowe Lieut. R.E. .... Rank.
for C.R.E. 1st Div.

1st. Division No. 95 (G)

Scheme of Training and of Organization for the First Division, during the period when it is in Reserve.

==================

1. The fighting which has been carried out by the 1st Division during the last six weeks, almost always with successful results, has caused some disorganization in companies and in battalions.

2. The fighting and hard work in the trenches have also resulted in some loss of efficiency, especially as regards that high standard of discipline which is essential in war.

3. During the period in reserve it is necessary for officers and non-commissioned officers of all ranks to apply themselves most strenuously to improve the efficiency of their Platoons, Companies, Battalions, and Brigades. Their attention must be particularly directed to the following objects:---

   (a). The tactical training of fire units, platoons, and companies.
   (b). The discipline of all ranks, the great object being to improve the moral and fighting efficiency of the Division.
   (c). The administration and interior economy of the Division.

4. Taking these three headings as a basis, the Major General Commanding wishes clearly to lay down first what is required to be done, and secondly how it is to be done. This will enable Brigade, Battalion, and Company Commanders to prepare definite programmes, and so to ensure that every moment of the day is turned to good account. WE have to improve the training, the discipline, and the moral of the men; not only by lectures indoors and by work on the ground, but by good food, by clean and comfortable billets, by amusements in the evening, and by a system for repairing clothing and equipment and for completing deficiencies, without making undue demands on the Ordnance which it is often impossible to meet in reasonable time.

5. It is proposed to deal with each of these headings in turn. Taking first the tactical training, the following are some of the many details which will readily occur to Company Commanders when instructing their platoon and fire-unit leaders.

   (a). We must first organize our fire-units under their own N.C.O.s so that each of the latter will become acquainted in a very few days with the military efficiency of every man under him. The same applies to platoon commanders: these officers and non-commissioned officers must get their men into hand, so that the whole body can be relied on to carry out intelligently and rapidly any operation they may be called upon to perform. They must be able to deploy quickly, to advance and to attack over any sort of ground without loss of cohesion or of direction, and to obey with the utmost promptitude any orders or signals they receive.

(b). Their fire discipline must be improved, and, so far as local circumstances will permit, every effort will be made to improve their shooting, especially as regards rapid fire.

(c). The men must be practised in digging trenches, one platoon competing against another with reference both to time and to the efficiency of the work.

(d). The men must be constantly practised in advancing out of a trench to the attack with the bayonet, covering a short distance to the enemy's trenches in an orderly manner and with the greatest possible rapidity.

(e). Practise is also necessary in bomb throwing, in the use of mortars, in advancing down a traversed trench to clear out an enemy with hand grenades, and in the use of Very's pistols. Every platoon will have a number of selected men who will be made especially proficient in these technical details.

(f). All kinds of devices for the improvement of trenches as regards their defence, capability of the most efficient fire on the enemy, protection from hostile fire, sanitation, and comfort, must be taught to the men.

(g). Special men must be selected for scouting and patrol work, and must constantly be practised in those duties both by day and by night.

(h). Selected good shots must be trained as "snipers", and must be taught how to act so as to deal efficiently with the enemy's snipers and to prevent the men in the enemy's trenches having a peaceful time.

[margin note: Selected observers among officers for reporting positions of enemy's trenches, new works & sniping posts]

There is a feeling amongst some Officers and men that the Germans are better at all sorts of dodges and devices than we are. There is no reason whatever for this belief, and when it exists it can easily be removed if fire unit and platoon commanders will display adequate ingenuity and initiative.

6.

6. In a similar manner battalion commanders must see that their companies are trained to act with precision and effect in any military operation, whether in the attack, or in the defence, or in the service of security. Their training must include the work of an ordinary outpost company, which they may at any time be called upon to perform, and of which we have had very little experience since the time when we arrived at the AISNE.

7. Battalion Commanders must also arrange for the training of machine gun detachments, of Battalion scouts and of stretcher bearers. Machine Gun Detachments must be trained in excess of immediate requirements, and in work with both Maxim and Vickers guns.

8. Brigade Commanders will arrange areas for Battalions, and Battalion Commanders for Companies. During the first week, which will be devoted to the training of fire units and of platoons, small areas only will be required. Digging grounds near the billets should be provided for every Battalion, and material should be bought on requisition through the R.E. for the construction of entanglements and of revetments, and for the improvement of wet trenches and the construction of loopholes.

9. Definite programmes of work will be prepared and will be adhered to by Battalion, Company, and Platoon Commanders each day's work being carefully mapped out beforehand.

10. To assist Officers in all this work, the G.O.C. 1st Division will hold a conference in each Brigade area twice a week, when all Officers of the Brigade and as many N.C.O.s, who are Platoon Commanders, as possible will attend.

11. DISCIPLINE may be considered under the following headings:---

(a). Self respect on the part of the individual, is created by scrupulous personal cleanliness, neatly trimmed hair, proper care of arms, equipment, and clothing, correct dress at all times, and a soldierly bearing.

(b). Smartness under arms, at drill, manoeuvres, and on fatigue duties, and general alertness and activity.

(c). The most careful and cheerful obedience of all orders received, and also of general instructions, such as sanitary rules in billets as regards food, bedding, cleanliness of floors, passages, and approaches to billets from the road, destruction and disposal of rubbish.

(d). Great attention to the proper manner of addressing and saluting officers, and speaking to N.C.O.s.

(e). Every effort must be made to reduce military offences by constant supervision on the part of officers and N.C.O.s so as to avoid the probability of crimes of the nature of disrespect, disobedience, acts of insubordination and drunkenness.

Both Officers and N.C.O.s are apt to become unduly impressed with the hardships that must be borne by the men during a campaign, and with the mistaken idea of ameliorating matters they only make the hardships greater by allowing small irregularities to go unchecked. There can be no excuse for this whilst the Division is in reserve.

(f). The men must have sufficient work but not too much. Long delays in "falling in", or long waits before the actual work in training must be avoided.

Three hours in the morning actual tactical training on the ground, and two hours in the afternoon devoted to drill, musketry, training specialists, improving muddy roads and approaches to billets, route marches to harden the men's feet, &c., is not too much provided the instruction is good, and the drill and fatigue work properly done.

(g). Amusements for the men after the day's work should be arranged by Battalion and Company Commanders. Football and other games such as rounders, sing-songs, concerts, boxing competitions are possible, with a little trouble and organization even in scattered billets. Everything that tends to make the men cheerful and happy is invaluable in war. Companies or platoons should be encouraged to whistle and sing when on the line of march. Any musical instruments which can be obtained such as drums, bugles, bag-pipes, mouth organs, &c., are very valuable.

12. The careful administration and interior economy of battalions and companies will go far to improve the military efficiency of the men.

Attention is required to the folowing point:--

(a). Cooking. Full use must be made of all the food provided, and the wastage caused partly by bad and unappetising cooking, and partly by the want of proper supervision by company officers and N.C.O.s and by neglect and carelessness of cooks and men themselves must be avoided.

A bowl of hot soup in billets when the men are going to bed would be greatly appreciated if it was properly made. The only reasons why soup is not available are that the cooks don't take the trouble to use up spare bones and vegetables, although there is plenty of such material and of kettles, which could be kept simmering on the fire all day and night.**

The cleanliness of cooking places is also important, especially the place where the meat is cut up. Ashes properly used will soon make a cooking place dry and healthy provided all water and refuse is properly disposed of. A refuse pit must be dug not too far from the kitchen, and all consumable refuse should be burnt in an incinerator.

(b). Washing places for men. In every billet arrangements must be made and a place told off where men can get hot water and have a good wash every day.

In addition to this, whenever possible, baths will be prepared under Divisional arrangements, and administered by Field Ambulances, where the men can get a thorough wash and have their clothes disinfected and cleaned.

(c). Care of Clothing and Equipment. There has been an enormous amount of waste owing to men throwing away articles of clothing and equipment simply because they are very dirty or somewhat worn; with the result that it has been quite impossible to meet the demands to replace losses. This applies to every article of clothing: shirts, socks, drawers, jerseys, boots, &c. Considerable wastage can be checked by demanding the return of every article which has to be replaced. Many of the articles thus withdrawn after washing or cleaning and mending are quite fit for re-issue.

Every battalion has tailors and shoemakers, and during the period the Division is in reserve extra assistants must be employed, and full use made of all these men.

During the last ten days 1069 pairs of boots which would otherwise have been thrown away have been repaired by regimental bootmakers working under Divisional arrangements in Bethune.

Much can be done towards the preservation of service dress clothing by ironing the jackets and trousers under company arrangements. Irons could be purchased out of company contingent funds.

(d). Care of billets. Attention is directed to the approaches to billets from the road so that mud should not be carried into the billets. These approaches should be cleaned up with twig brooms. Straw mats can easily be made to put on the threshold and other similar mats outside each room. All cleaning up of billets to be done before breakfast.

The straw bedding should be shaken up every morning and put back near the wall; all small bits of straw left on the

** It is very easy for the Sergnt.Cook or C.Q.Sergt. to say that the men don't care for it-which is the usual reason given-but the real truth is that no one bothers about it.

ground, and all dust and dirt must ~~be swept outside~~ the rooms and carried out of doors and burnt.

The passages and staircases must be kept properly clean. Clean paths should be prepared leading to the latrines, and urinals must be dug just outside the billet for use at night only.

Stable refuse and litter must not be allowed to accumulate in the neighbourhood of transport or other horses, but must be removed daily to some selected spot.

All billets must be inspected daily by an Officer to see that these instructions are properly carried out.

(c). <u>Precautions against fire.</u> Before going into new billets men must be cautioned as to what steps are to be taken to avoid risk of fire, &c., where it is safe to hang lamps or place candles; whether smoking is allowed; where cooking is to be done; whether braziers are to be allowed, &c.

13. <u>Care of property of inhabitants.</u>
Complaints are constantly received from owners of billets against the troops billeted on them. These are generally due to men helping themselves to straw, firewood, and vegetables. This practise must not be allowed on any pretext, and all issues must be made under the supervision of an Officer from the source indicated by the Area Requisitioning Officer.

Before the troops enter the billet, the condition of the billet must be noted by a company officer, and when tactical considerations permit the same officer should accompany the Officer around the billet before the troops move off and assure himself that no damage has been done to the property. Minor breakages or damages of a similar nature must be paid for by him and a receipt obtained for the amount.

Gate posts, fence rails, gates, and hop-poles are on no account to be used for firewood without the order of an officer, who will report in writing, through the usual channel, the paricular circumstances of the case.

(14). <u>Behaviour towards the inhabitants.</u>
All ranks should remember that long-continued billeting of troops is very irksome to the inhabitants, and that they must endeavour by their general behaviour to ease the burden as much as they can.

E.S. HOARE NAIRNE, Colonel,
General Staff, 1st Divn.

30th January, 1915.

With reference to circular memorandum, 1st Div. No. 95 of 30=1=15 the following additional instructions are issued--

5 (c). A uniform type of trench should be adopted which will suit most localities, and it is considered that (1) traverses six feet long by four feet wide should be placed at intervals of eighteen feet. (2). Whatever the section of trench may be good firing positions must be given so that fire can be delivered over the parapet, a firm footing for each man being essential. <u>Loopholes.</u> Should be provided for snipers and sentries only. When possible loophole plates are to be used, and these should be sloped slightly backwards at the top.

(3). As material for trench work such as sandbags is difficult to obtain owing to requirements at the front, the demands for practice should be kept as low as possible, and material should be used over again as much as can be managed. Demands should be sent to the   Field Company R.E. at

(e). A few Officers and N.C.O.s in each battalion should act as instructors in bomb throwing, and instructions for these can be given by the   Field Company if required.

9th February, 1915.
Lieut. Colonel,
C.R.E., First Division.

1st Divn No 95(G.)

C.R.E.
1st Divn.

Attached are copies of the memos which will go to Infantry Brigadiers this evening containing the instructions which you drafted on the subject of trenches, loopholes, material, & instruction of bomb-throwers. The paragraph on the instruction of bomb-throwers has been slightly altered from your draft, in accordance with our conversation.

Will you inform the OsC of 23rd & 26th Field Coys of the arrangement?

E.S. Hoare Nairne
Lt Col GS.
1st Divn

11 Feb. 1915.

Copy.   1st Divn. No. 95 (G.)

1st Guards Brigade.

r/30-1-15

With reference to circular memorandum, 1st Div. No.95, the following additional instructions are issued:—

5 (c). A uniform type of trench should be adopted which will suit most localities, and it is considered that (1) traverses six feet long by four feet wide should be placed at intervals of eighteen feet. (2). Whatever the section of trench may be good firing positions must be given so that fire can be delivered over the parapet, a firm footing for each man being essential. Loopholes. Should be provided for snipers and sentries only. When possible loophole plates are to be used, and these should be sloped slightly backwards at the top.

(3). As material for trench work such as sandbags is difficult to obtain owing to requirements at the front, the demands for practice should be kept as low as possible, and material should be used over again as much as can be managed. Demands should be sent to the 28th Field Company R.E. at HURIONVILLE

(c). At least one officer and 4 N.C.os in each Battalion should be trained to act as instructors in bomb throwing. The training of these instructors will be carried out by the 28th Field Company, R.E., under arrangements to be made directly between the Headquarters, 1st Guards Brigade, and the O.C. 28th Field Company, R.E.

E. Hoare Nairne.
Lieut. Colonel,
Gen Staff. First Division.

4th February, 1915.

1st. Divn. No. 95 (G).

2nd Infantry Brigade.
3rd Infantry Brigade.

Copy

With reference to circular memorandum, 1st Div. No.95 the following additional instructions are issued—

(c). A uniform type of trench should be adopted which will suit most localities, and it is considered that (1) traverses six feet long by four feet wide should be placed at intervals of eighteen feet. (2). Whatever the section of trench may be good firing positions must be given so that fire can be delivered over the parapet, a fire footing for each man being essential. <u>Loopholes.</u> Should be provided for snipers and sentries only. When possible loophole plates are to be used, and these should be sloped slightly backwards at the top.

(3). As material for trench work such as sandbags is difficult to obtain owing to requirements at the front, the demands for practice should be kept as low as possible, and material should be used over again as much as can be managed. Demands should be sent to the 26th Field Company R.E. at LA PUGNOY

(e). At least one officer and 4 N.C.O's in each Battalion should be trained to act as instructors in bomb throwing. The training of these instructors will be carried out by the 26th Field Company, R.E., under arrangements to be made directly between the Headquarters, of {2nd/3rd} Infantry Brigade, and the O.C. 26th Field Company, R.E.

E. Hoare Nairne.
Lieut. Colonel,
Gen. Staff First Division.

11th February, 1915.

1st Division No. 131 (G).

1st D.E. (For information).

The attached notes on wire entanglements are forwarded for the guidance of infantry officers in command of sub-sections of defence.

1st Div. H.Q.
13th February 1915.

B. Lefroy Captain.
General Staff, 1st Division.

3 copies retained for field corps

C.H.B.

NOTES ON WIRE ENTANGLEMENTS.

LOW WIRE ENTANGLEMENT.

A tendency has been observed to make low wire entanglements on too regular a pattern, the result being that they are very easy to pass through.

A low obstacle is used, (a) in order to come as a surprise to the enemy, and, (b) so as not to disclose the position of the work it covers. Without breaking these conditions the entanglement, may be rendered far more efficient by the addition of <u>loose</u> strands of barbed wire, and these should be copiously provided. In cases where the formation of the ground renders part of the obstacle invisible to the enemy until they are close upon it, a single line of high apron fence through the centre of the obstacle would be of great value.

CONCEALMENT FROM AEROPLANES.

Tops of newly cut stakes should be at once smeared with mud, and any opportunity should be taken to conceal the obstacle by natural or artificial means.

DEPTH OF OBSTACLE.

The depth of a low entanglement should never be less than 15 feet.

BLOCKING ROADS.

*(Reseaux Brun)

When French wire obstacle* is used to block a road, a single line does not make an efficient obstacle, even when strengthened by strands of barbed wire (and this should invariably be done). Two or three coils should be used at such a distance apart that a rush will not carry men through more than one at a time. If possible, the obstacles should be sited so that one cannot be seen from another.

IN FRONT OF FIRE TRENCHES.

Where the tactical situation renders ordinary work impossible, no effort should be spared to gradually build us efficient protection, by continually strengthening and adding to such obstacles as it may be possible to fix. Many devices are in use, such as, strengthened French obstacle, barbed wire wound in a similar manner to the French obstacle, iron or wooden frames covered with wire and connected by loose strands. Every obstacle of this nature, after being pushed out in position, should be gradually improved and strengthened, by the addition of loose strands, etc.

It should not be necessary to add that every portion of an obstacle should be under the close rifle fire of the defenders.

Letters of Appreciation

1st Division No. 130 (G).

C.R.E.

I am directed by the Major General Commanding to send you 5 copies of 1st Division Memorandum No.130 (G), conveying to you and to the troops under your command his thanks and his appreciation of the work which has been carried out since the 1st Division arrived near LA BASSÉE.

I also enclose 5 copies of similar memoranda, which have been sent to the Royal Artillery and to the Infantry of the Division, and in which the Major General is certain that the Sappers will heartily concur.

1st Div. H.Q.
12th February 1915.

E. Hoare Nairne.
Lieut. Colonel.
General Staff, 1st Division.

More copies are available if you would care for them.

E.H.N.

1st Division No. 130/2 (G).

C. R. E.
    1st Division.

    The Major General Commanding wishes to thank the C.R.E., 1st Division and the Company Commanders for their able assistance during the last six weeks fighting.

    When, by their attacks on the 21st and 22nd December, the troops of the 1st Division had gained possession of the GIVENCHY - FESTUBERT line, the only cover available was certain lengths of old communication trench, which were neither continuous nor traversed. The work done by the Royal Engineers on the 21st and 22nd December and on the days immediately following, in planning and supervising the construction of a connected line of defence, was of supreme value to the troops.

    The enterprise of detachments of Royal Engineers in placing wire in front of our trenches and in gaps, in many instances in close proximity to the enemy, and in planning and superintending the construction of trenches in advance of our front line by the process of "jumping" has contributed very largely to the constant improvement of our front line of defence.

    The skill with which the Royal Engineers sited and designed the works in close support of the front line, and the energy with which they ############ directed their construction has been a main factor in the successes gained by the Division.

    The Major General wishes to express to all ranks of the R.E. his appreciation, which is shared by higher authorities, of the good work which has been mentioned above, but especially also of the steady continuous service, both by way of supervision and of actual work, which they have done in the fire trenches and communication trenches during a long period of exceptionally bad weather. This service has entailed severe physical strain, and the fact that it has been carried on with only a small sick return testifies to the high state of the spirit and of the interior economy of the Royal Engineer companies.

    The Royal Engineers, who have so largely aided the successful actions of the Infantry and Artillery during the last six weeks, can look forward with confidence to their part in still more successful offensive action in the future, and thus to helping the Division to do its full share in bringing the campaign to a successful conclusion.

E.J. Hoare Travine

1st Division H.Q.
11th February 1915.
                         Lieut. Colonel.
                   General Staff, 1st Division.

Infantry Brigades, Battalions, and Companies in the Division, after their successful experiences during the last six weeks, which have gained the thanks of Sir John French, and which have involved far more heavy fighting than in any other part of the British Line, can look forward with confidence to still more successful offensive action in the future, and thus ensure that the Division will do its full share in bringing the campaign to an early and successful conclusion.

It only rests with us now, to continue the training of the new officers and men who have arrived to fill our ranks, to get to know the capabilities of each man, and do our utmost to maintain the high standard of discipline which already exists in the Division, thus strengthening and increasing our powers of attack.

E.S. Hoare Nairne.

1st Division H.Q.
11th February 1915.

Lieut. Colonel.
General Staff, 1st Division.

1st Division No.130 (G).

The Major General Commanding the Division wishes to express to General Officers Commanding Infantry Brigades his deep appreciation, which is shared by higher authorities, of the excellent work done by them during the last six weeks' fighting.

In spite of the constant strain on Brigade Commanders and their Staff, due to the many attacks made by us and by the enemy during this period, they have never relaxed their efforts to ensure success.

The attacks carried out by all the Infantry Brigades of the Division in the most difficult circumstances on the 21st and 22nd December reflect the greatest credit upon all ranks, and ensured the re-establishment of the defence of GIVENCHY and FESTUBERT and the line further north at a most critical time.

The attack of the 1st Guards Brigade, which was exceptionally difficult, owing to the fall of GIVENCHY, on which the right flank of the attack was hinged, will stand out as a brilliant achievement.

The defence of GIVENCHY by the 3rd Brigade on 25th January, the success of which was due to the carefully laid plans of the Brigade Commander, and to the immediate and vigorous counter-strokes delivered by Battalion and Company Commanders and carried out with such fine spirit by the men, is a splendid example of an offensive defence.

The defence of CUINCHY also by the 2nd Brigade on 29th January and the numerous attacks made by the Brigade against the enemy's posts on the railway embankment, the constant change of the line of defence, involving the most strenuous work on the part of the men in constructing new trenches, are fine examples of what can be done by British troops. The work in the trenches has been very hard, the weather conditions have been exceptionally bad, and it is a matter of the highest satisfaction to every Battalion, Company, and Platoon in the Division that they have been able to retain the true offensive spirit throughout.

The excellent work done by snipers and patrols, both by day and night, has broken down the fire power of the enemy, and has kept him in constant dread of an attack, while it has created a feeling of security amongst our own troops.

The service of inter-communication has been very efficiently maintained by the Signal Company and Brigade and Battalion orderlies; credit is specially due to the linesmen and orderlies, who, often under a heavy fire, have ensured the rapid transmission of messages.

In all this work the infantry have been most ably supported by the artillery and engineers, to whom the Major General has sent a separate memorandum, which is attached, and which he knows will be cordially endorsed by all ranks in the Infantry.

1st Division No. 130/1 (G).

G.O.C., R.A.
   1st Division.

    The Major General Commanding the Division wishes to place on record his appreciation, which is shared by higher authorities, of the excellent work done by the Artillery of all ranks throughout the six weeks' operations near LA BASSEE. There has never before been such close co-operation between the Artillery and Infantry; and it is probable that these operations will stand out in the future as an example of what it is possible to do when Infantry and Artillery Commanders work together so constantly to gain a definite objective.

    The system which has been adopted by the artillery to bring about these most desirable results has been tested both in attack and defence and proved to be highly effective.

    The General Officer Commanding wishes to thank the G.O.C., R.A., of the Division and the Artillery Brigade and Battery Commanders for initiating and carrying out successfully this comprehensive scheme of operations. He also wishes to thank the Observing Officers who have done splendid work in their forward observing stations right in the Infantry line. The Batteries also by their efficient fire discipline and their careful and accurate laying and fuze setting, both by day and night, have done their full share in producing such excellent results, and the Brigade and Divisional Ammunition Columns have never failed in the supply of ammunition.

    Great praise is due to the Artillery signallers for their strenuous work, often under heavy fire, in maintaining communication over all parts of the battlefield and especially between the forward observing stations and the Brigades and Batteries, where the lines were constantly cut.

    The General Officer Commanding also wishes to thank all ranks for the very valuable information that has been obtained by the Artillery and transmitted rapidly from all parts of the firing line, and which has materially helped him in the conduct of the operations. He has no doubt that the valuable experience gained by the Artillery during the past six weeks will be of great use to them when our army commences to advance, and when, instead of the operations being of the nature of trench fighting, every one will be moving, and communication and co-operation will be more difficult.

1st Division H.Q.
11th February 1915.

                            Lieut. Colonel.
                  General Staff, 1st Division.

WAR DIARY

G.O.C. 1st DIVISION

March

1918

Army Form C. 2118.

WAR DIARY
or
INTELLIGENCE SUMMARY. H.Q. 1st DIVISIONAL ENGINEERS
(Erase heading not required.) — MARCH 1915 —

No. 8.

Instructions regarding War Diaries and Intelligence Summaries are contained in F.S.Regs., Part II. and the Staff Manual respectively. Title pages will be prepared in manuscript.

Hour, Date, Place	Summary of Events and Information	Remarks and references to Appendices
HINGES. 1.3.15 (Monday)	Division Headquarters have asked for approaches to be constructed. A wire was sent to 1st Corps, who replied that they ended do the work. (R.E. 38) C.R.E. visited 1st Bde. Section returning at 10.30 p.m.	Daily Progress Reports showing the work carried out by each Fd. Co. A statement showing the stores received each day from the R.E. Park & distributed to Companies, and a statement showing the daily progress made in Mining are attached hereto as well as (a reference from) the messages received (see Q and next sht.) R4. R13. R37. R2. R3 A4. Q.991 R7. Q. RE43. R9. 1141. 1519, 1949, R9, R10.
2.3.15 5.30 a.m	Capt. Richard returned from leave & resumed the duties of Adjt. 2/Lt. Ross rejoined 26th Co.	
9.30	C.R.E. visited 26th Co. Following documents rec'd :- 1st Dn. N° 1121 Repairs of Roads & Bridges. 157 (G) Notes on area occupied by German VII Corps (SECRET)	

Army Form C. 2118.

WAR DIARY
or
INTELLIGENCE SUMMARY.
(Erase heading not required.)

Instructions regarding War Diaries and Intelligence Summaries are contained in F.S. Regs., Part II. and the Staff Manual respectively. Title pages will be prepared in manuscript.

Hour, Date, Place	Summary of Events and Information	Remarks and references to Appendices
HINGES		
3-3-15 (Wednesday)	Adjutant with 1 lorry to BOIS DE PACAULT to arrange about supply of hurdles.	E 56, E 57, R 8
	C.R.E. & Adjutant to 23rd Co. in afternoon & went round 2nd line breastworks in Section D.	R 8, R 11, K 8, R 12
	Following secret memos received —	E 59, K 9, E 60
	1st Divn No. 158 (G) Reorganization of Artillery	
	——— 153 (G) Information regarding plans etc. not to be given to liaison officers	
	Statement showing distribution of Infantry Battalions.	
	Also	
	1st Divn No. 150 (G) — Use of Rifle Grenades & methods of firing Rifle.	
	C.R.E. asked C.E., 1 Corps H.Q. (with plate) on use of German hand mines rec'd.	
	Message from Works G.H.Q. stating that Ordnance have been asked to increase supply of sand bags.	
4-3-15	Adjutant in lorry to STRAZEELE to enquire into supply of	Q 81, W 802

WAR DIARY
or
INTELLIGENCE SUMMARY.
(Erase heading not required.)

Army Form C. 2118.

Hour, Date, Place	Summary of Events and Information	Remarks and references to Appendices
HINGES		
4-3-15 (Thursday) cont.d	Sand bags & revetting materials.	
	CRE visited 23rd Co. to select a name near Hinges A.	E 61
	2 horses were employed in transport of hurdles from BOIS DE	
	PACAUT to 23rd & 26th Cos.	E 62 RB 9 R 15 R 16
	Captain Ball R.E. left for England 15 day and Bt. Major	R 17 D6 2 RB 12 K 15
	Dobbs R.E. took over command of 1st Sig. Co.	L 15 980
	1st Div M/159 (G) – Notes re mining operations received from French.	
5-3-15	CRE visited 23rd & 26th Co.	JR 1 JR 1½ K 16
	Signal Co. Lorry sent to St Cigale for stores	R 20 R 21 JR 2
	By French Rockets received from DiArt., were sent to 26th Fd.	
	Co. to experiment with.	
	Conducting parties sent to CHOCQUES, in accordance with instructions	
	received from 1st Divn., at 3 p.m., arrived HINGES 8.30 p.m.	
	bringing horses as under, which were handed over to representatives	
	of Companies :– 23rd Co. 4 Heavy Draught	JR 3 JR 4 Ca 12
	26th 1	SC 205 JR 5 JR 7
	1 light	B 996 Ca 8

Army Form C. 2118.

WAR DIARY
or
INTELLIGENCE SUMMARY.
(Erase heading not required.)

(4)

Hour, Date, Place	Summary of Events and Information	Remarks and references to Appendices
HINGES		
5-3-15 (Friday) (Continued)	Brick Factory, having received a supply of Hyposcope from Pat. Park, was instructed to issue 1 to 6 Veterans to 1st Div Co., 9 Maxim to 23rd Co. & the remaining 10 to 26th Co.	
6.3.15	Adj. visited Bout Factory to arrange about (a) Special (Anvil) mining Casing, (b) Timbers for a bridge to take led horses, (c) earth trucks, (d) sand-bags.	JR 11 E 63
	2.15 Co. having reported that a dismounted Sergt. had been sent to Hinges instead of a mounted Sergt. (who is badly needed) Records were asked to adjust the matter as soon as possible.	JR 19 RE 42 E 64
		RB 4 1087
	10–11.5 A.M. a message (ZA 41) from 1st Bde to 1st Div was rec'd stating that "Reuter" extra had placed report to Colsterworm that mining going on just East of Princes Road salient & every certainty under works at this point." CRE tel'd to Div's AG to discuss the situation	1st Div order N° 64
		JR 16 RB 6 JR 15
		JR 17 1021 JR 14
	Decided that immediate action should be left to the RE officer (Major Russell Brown) on the spot.	JR 20 X K 22
		ZA 41
	1st Div. order N° 64 – Relief of B.D. by 2nd Bde.	

WAR DIARY or INTELLIGENCE SUMMARY

Army Form C. 2118.

Hour, Date, Place	Summary of Events and Information	Remarks and references to Appendices
HINGES	(5)	
7-3-15 (Sunday)	CRE to 23rd Co. at 8.15 a.m. to arrange for countermining	1031 JR 21
10.15 a.m.	Message from CRE stating that the supply of at least 2 pumps is urgent. Abt. telephoned to 2nd Dn. ? Bond Factory; tried to struggle; JR 24 JR 25 JR 27 & enquired through 1st Divn. Hd. Welsh Bdes. had any pumps available. R72 R2 Ca 5 Bond Factory promised 2 pumps by Monday evening; enquiries of the E 65 JR 26 JR 29 other places enumerated were fruitless. Further enquiring into last nights alarm about mining rather discredited JR 28 JR 29 Q 1448 the statement made in the message. Arrangements were however made JR 31 Q 151 RE 279 to push on with the countermining to refill as possible 23rd & 28th. The L 32 P 257 Co. was each to sink a shaft & 1st Hunland Co. 2 shafts. The personnel available for this work comprised the two locally formed sections at 170/15 Co. RE. (No. 1 Section attached 23rd Co., No. 2 Section attached 28th Co.) Each section comprised 1 officer & about 50 O.R. Captain visited D.A.D.O.S. in afternoon & arranged for a supply of rejoined clothing & gum boots to be issued to mining sections.	

WAR DIARY
or
INTELLIGENCE SUMMARY.
(Erase heading not required.)

Army Form C. 2118.

Instructions regarding War Diaries and Intelligence Summaries are contained in F.S. Regs., Part II. and the Staff Manual respectively. Title pages will be prepared in manuscript.

Hour, Date, Place	Summary of Events and Information	Remarks and references to Appendices
HINGES	(6)	
8-3-15 (Monday)	In accordance with 1st Corps instructions, 6 specially enlisted tunnelling from 2nd Divn were posted to the mining section attached to 23rd Co	JR 32
The following documents were received this day to field :—	No "supply" lorries being available, the Signal Co lorry was borrowed last to Strazeele for stores.	
First 1st Army { Notes on F.G.C.E. Mantel {Requisitioning & Billeting	C.R.E. remained at Headquarters to deal with correspondence – especially that relating to the formation of mining sections.	JR 33 RE 43
		G 363 E 66
1st Divn No. 166(G) Use of Screens	C.R.E. visited 28th & 1st Husband Fd. Co.	JR 34 46 JR 35
Telescope & periscope in German trenches.	A very good tunnelling report was on the French Rockets issued for experimental purposes to 26th Co was forwarded to Dist HQ.	(A)
Orders for Contact Posts – French Traffic – Passes – Civilians etc.	1st Corps were asked about the quantity & location of spare bridging equipment.	
	C.R.E. applied to 1st Divn for 25 miners to complete the 2 mining Sections up to Establishment; these were sent at 6 p.m.	E 67
	R.E. Park were asked to supply from more Pumps, high & Force, for use in connection with mining	E 66 JR 2 JR 1
	1st Corps notified the opening (on 11th inst) of R.E Park at Beyuette.	JR 3 GR4
		G 2136 105 2

WAR DIARY
or
INTELLIGENCE SUMMARY.
(Erase heading not required.)

Army Form C. 2118.

(7)

Hour, Date, Place	Summary of Events and Information	Remarks and references to Appendices
HINGES		
9-3-15 (Tuesday)	C.R.E. visited Div. H.Q. & subsequently proceeded to 26th 123rd Co. 2 hours went to Strazeele for R.E. stores & intend to have put forward an urgent appeal for 2 pumps, light & trams, 26th Co. were asked to let Stan have a couple, they being subsequently did. Orders were received this evening that the 12th Army would carry out an attack tomorrow (1st Div's Order N° 65) (a Tactical report in LILLE was received & copies were circulated to units. Secret instructions from 1st Div's regarding defensive lines in rear of our position was received.	B 32 JR 9 JR 8 JR 10 JR 11 P.Dw 12 168.(c) B 35 Cy 3 RB 2 RB 3 1074 JR 17 JR 16
10.3.15 (Wednesday) 7.15 am	C.R.E. to Report Centre (le Hamel) and remained there all day. Coly joined him there at 9.45 - visited 28th & howitzer Co & returned to HINGES at 2 pm Three "Supply" lorries were allotted this morning for R.E. stores & were despatched 1 to STRAZEELE & 2 to BERGUETTE. The STRAZEELE one broke down enroute & returned empty.	16 82 JR 20 G-317 JR 14 10 857 L5 1337 PE/ 503 G 328 RE 46 A 216 A 219

Army Form C. 2118.

WAR DIARY
or
INTELLIGENCE SUMMARY.
(Erase heading not required.)

Instructions regarding War Diaries and Intelligence Summaries are contained in F.S. Regs., Part II. and the Staff Manual respectively. Title pages will be prepared in manuscript.

Hour, Date, Place	Summary of Events and Information	Remarks and references to Appendices
HINGES		
11.3.15 (Thursday)	A sudden demand for hand tools having arisen, CRE motored to Bruce Factory at midnight & brought out 300 hand tools to 23rd Co. CRE to Report Centre at 7 A.M.; visited 26th Co. 9.30, returning to Report Centre at 11 a.m. Adj. to Report Centre at 10 a.m. Visited 23rd & Riverland Co. 3 p.m., returning HINGES 5 p.m. CRE to 26th Co. 3 p.m. & returned to HINGES 5.30 p.m. Application was made this morning to 1st Div. for 8 motorcycles for the use of the officers of Mining Sections. (JR 23)	D3 G 322 JR 23 JR 26 G(x) 2 JR 21 X JR 25 M1 JR 29 Ca 5 JR 30 39 OE 47 Q 235 RE 503 JR 31 JR 33 JR 32 11.25 52
12.3.15. 11.30 a.m.	Major H.W. Weekes R.E. reported to for duty with 1st D.E.; he proceeded at midday with the C.R.E. to Report Centre. CRE visited 26th Co. & returned to HINGES at 5 p.m. One lorry sent to BERGUETTE & 1 to BOIS DE PACAULT to bring handles for 26th Co. Report (JR1) to 1st Corps showing 6 Pontoons & 2 Trestles & bridge near GORRE; 2 Trestles with superstructure afloat with 26th Co. 1st Div. notified (Q 243) that 1 man was due CHOCQUE'S about 3 p.m.	G 444 JR 36 JR 87 JR 38 JR 1: 1137 57 Q 243 G 351 G 355 Q 258 JR 2 JR 4 W 10 G 378 Q 264 G 376

Army Form C. 2118.

WAR DIARY
or
INTELLIGENCE SUMMARY.
(Erase heading not required.)

Instructions regarding War Diaries and Intelligence Summaries are contained in F.S. Regs., Part II. and the Staff Manual respectively. Title pages will be prepared in manuscript.

Hour, Date, Place	Summary of Events and Information	Remarks and references to Appendices
HINGES		
13.3.15 (Saturday)	C.R.E. with Major Weekes to Report Centre & subsequently visited 23rd How. Co. 2 horses went to BERGUETTE. A plan of the area near FOURNES – AUBERS – NEUVE-CHAPELLE was received.	JR 3 JR 5 1147 68 M 1052 78 RE 51 W 11 R138 R137 G 401 JR 9 M 1059 JR 12
14-3-15	C.R.E. with Major Weekes to 26th Co. & went round trenches at FESTUBERT with General HEATH. Adj. with Davies to BERGUETTE to make arrangements about supply of sand bags, which had been latterly been unsatisfactory.	E 70 RE 52 JR 14 RE 53 Co. 2 JR 15 RB 6 JR 18 Y RE 55 JR 19
15.3.15	C.R.E. & Major Weekes to 23rd Co. at 9.30 a.m. & reconnoitred track across fields for new road to be constructed by 23rd Co.; subsequently went round trenches in D Section, going up via DEAD COW FARM & returning via INDIAN VILLAGE. 2 horses to BERGUETTE. Adj. to Bour Factory & confirmed the arrangement that 500 sand bags should be supplied daily to 2/1 F.C. Adj. visited 26th Co. in afternoon. C.R.E.'s report giving nominal rolls of women (N.Z. & S.Z. Sections) attached to 23rd & 26th Co. forwarded to 1st Division.	E 73 JR 23 JR 22 87 91 G 412 BDE OS 56 G 415 L 25 1183 1184 JR 27 192 E 75

Army Form C. 2118.

WAR DIARY
or
INTELLIGENCE SUMMARY.
(Erase heading not required.)

Hour, Date, Place	Summary of Events and Information	Remarks and references to Appendices
HINGES 15-3-15 (Monday) Contd	Lieut. BARCLAY, lent from 2nd D.E., returned to CAMBRIN 1st morning. This officer came originally from 2nd Divn. with the 6 specially enlisted miners belonging to 2 B.G.s Mining Section (No.) Memo (1st Corps No. 2/30) received directing that indents for extra cyclists for mining sections should be put forward; noted & returned to 1st Division. Captain Forsyth R.A.M.C. transferred to No 2 Field Ambulance & replaced at HQ 1st D.E. by Lieut. J.S. Lloyd R.A.M.C. from No 1 F.A. 1st Division asked (CR 23) to arrange for 3rd Bde. to supply 8 miners to No 2 Section to replace casualties & bring up to strength. C.R.E. arranged (CR 75) for 30 cyclists (Div. Mtd Tps) to be at 23rd C.I. Billets at to morrow morning to assist in making road near RICHEBOURG.	(10) E 74 H

WAR DIARY
or
INTELLIGENCE SUMMARY.
(Erase heading not required.)

Army Form C. 2118.

Instructions regarding War Diaries and Intelligence Summaries are contained in F. S. Regs., Part II. and the Staff Manual respectively. Title pages will be prepared in manuscript.

Hour, Date, Place	Summary of Events and Information	Remarks and references to Appendices
HINGES		
16-5-15 (Tuesday)	C.R.E. & Major Weekes motored out to 26th Co. billets; returned to see G.O.C. but as he had gone out, they went out again & visited 2nd & 3rd Homeland Fd. Co. on the road - RICHEBOURG. Signal Co. hurry went to Bourette Rd at 9 am, followed later by two 2-lm lorries from Supply Column. M.Dur. № 170 (G) (SECRET) circulated to companies. Copy of German Instructions for construction of defensive positions circulated to Companies. C.R.E., on his return saw the General with reference to defences on right of C. Section. C.R.E. addressed a message (JR 6) to Maj. General Rice. On the restricted supply of sand bags recently received. Note on Field Defences made this MDWP № 232 (G) - vs training to wipe.	101 Co 1 RB 3 JR 2 JR 29 RE 4+9 DAY N B 72 G 424 JR 28 C/52 JRC JR 7 JR 8 1/0 G 426
17.5.15	C.R.E. to headquarters & then rode out to 2nd B to Rode out with Major Lewis to ST HUBERT & went into formal trenches on right. Its C.R.E. accompanied G.O.C. to advance with 2nd DIVS in BETHUNE at 5.30 pm 3 horses to BERGUETTE	⊗ IRO RB 2 RE 58 RO 4 OR 14 JR 12 JR 4 RB 6 RS c/103 G 11 & 317 JR 13 G.14 R.F.6.

(73989) W4141-463. 400,000. 9/14. H.&J.Ltd. Forms/C. 2118/10.

Army Form C. 2118.

WAR DIARY
or
INTELLIGENCE SUMMARY.
(Erase heading not required.)

Instructions regarding War Diaries and Intelligence Summaries are contained in F.S. Regs., Part II and the Staff Manual respectively. Title pages will be prepared in manuscript.

Hour, Date, Place	Summary of Events and Information	Remarks and references to Appendices
HINGES 18-3-15 (Thursday)	CRE visited Headquarters & subsequently went round to all three Fd Companies & to 1st FB.d Bde Headquarters. Adjutant to BETHUNE & brought small stores for 23rd Co. Adj. visited 23rd Co. at 4 p.m. Indent for 4 motor cycles was sent to Adv.d MT. Depôt ROUEN. These Cycles are for the use of Officers of Mining Sections.	139 JR 22 JR 20 D B 352 2224 a 264 M 3049 145
19-3-15 (Friday)	CRE to 26th Co. & visited right of C section with reference to Strengthening Point A. Captain SYMINGTON & Lieut MARSDEN 1st Husband Co. proceeded on leave of absence to SCOTLAND until 27th inst. 3 Lorries to R.E. Park BERGUETTE. Arrangements were made to issue Green overalls/clothing to all Field Companies R.E. Records Box were asked to (JR 2) to supply a mounted N.C.O. for R.E. Co.	145 RE 64 RE 55 JR 31 1235 JR 6 RE 66 Ca 1 JR 36 D1 X Cy 12 JR 37 a 376 Ca 15 JR 2

WAR DIARY
or
INTELLIGENCE SUMMARY.
(Erase heading not required.)

Army Form C. 2118.

Hour, Date, Place	Summary of Events and Information	Remarks and references to Appendices
HINGES 20-3-15 (Saturday)	C.R.E visited all three Field Companies & horses proceeded to R.E. Park. 2/Lieut. SEABROOK proceeded to ENGLAND on leave of absence to 28th inst. 1st Div. No. 1301 recd. — Notifies that N.C.Os of Territorial Force doing duty with Regular Units are to be in the same footing for pension etc as Regular N.C.O's 1st Div. No. 1299 — Contact, etc, of R.E. Parks transferred to Armies. 1st Div. No. 1295 — Cameras to be sent home. Sapper STEVENSON (C.R.E's Orderly) sent to Base for Transfer to Signal Service & replaced by Spr TURNER from 26th Co. 6 Pumps, lift 18 Force & were received from R.E. Park. 2 Petrol driven Pumps were received by 26th Co. from 2nd Div. & arrangements were made for a supply of petrol & oil. C.R.E had arranged to interview Engineer N.C.Os etc. and candidates proposed for Commissions in Mining Cos from R.E. but had to postpone it on account of the necessity of arranging for taking over a new portion of the Line in the neighbourhood of NEUVE CHAPELLE.	(13) Cas E. IR 15 166 IR 18 215 Ptes (3) E 19 IR 80 395 (X) IR 23 L 20 The following were received from H.Q. 1st Division — 1st Div. No. 1295 — Cameras due to precaution to be observed as "killed in action" 1st Div. No. 30ff. Pressure of air from gauge gine etc 1st Div. No. 175(5) R. Pyromade with Bangalore Torpedoes

Army Form C. 2118.

WAR DIARY
or
INTELLIGENCE SUMMARY.
(Erase heading not required.)

Instructions regarding War Diaries and Intelligence Summaries are contained in F.S. Regs., Part II. and the Staff Manual respectively. Title pages will be prepared in manuscript.

Hour, Date, Place	Summary of Events and Information	Remarks and references to Appendices
HINGES	(14)	
21-3-15 (Sunday)	C.R.E. & Major WEEKES to billets of LAHORE D.E. at [crossed out] round trenches (near NEUVE CHAPELLE) with a view to taking over this portion of the line.	A 17 A 23 JR 24
	2 horses to R.E. Park.	E 22 H 2 (A) (B)
	Adj. visited 23rd & 1st husband & billets	RE 523 JR 27
	Arrangements were made (R.E. 528) for 2nd D.B. & Bde. men to man 1st Civilian labour employed in C section.	
	1st Div. No 1285 recd — Instructions regarding Trade Test in active Service	
	1st Div. No 1318 ---- — Defective Hand Grenades.	
22-3-15	CRE to RUE DE BOIS & went round trenches there with a view to taking over; subsequently visited 1st husband, 23rd & 26th Co.	G 447 A 223 JR 34
	A translation of some German Bde. & Reg. orders regarding the preparation of Tates of wire etc, were received from 1st Divn & was circulated to units.	
	A report by Major LEWIS on the German Trenches in front of FESTUBERT was submitted (with sketch) to General Staff	
	1st Div's Order No 714 recd. 9.30 p.m.	

Army Form C. 2118.

WAR DIARY
or
INTELLIGENCE SUMMARY.
(Erase heading not required.)

Instructions regarding War Diaries and Intelligence Summaries are contained in F.S. Regs., Part II. and the Staff Manual respectively. Title pages will be prepared in manuscript.

Hour, Date, Place	Summary of Events and Information	Remarks and references to Appendices
HINGES 21-3-15 (Sunday)	(14) C.R.E. & Major WEEKES to billets of LAHORE D.S. at [illegible] & went round trenches (near NEUVE CHAPELLE) with a view to taking over the portion of the line & horses to R.E. Park. Adj: visited 23rd & 1st hundred & billets Arrangements were made (R.E.S.23) for 2nd D.S. to take over to morrow 1 E Civilian Labour employed in C. Section 1st O wt No 1823 rec'd — Instructions regarding Trade Tests on active Service 1st O wt No 1318 — — Defective Hand Grenades	A 17 A 23 JR 24 E 22 Y 2 (A) (B) RE 523 JR 27 [illegible]
22-3-15	C.R.E. to RUE DE BOIS & went round trenches there with a view to taking over; Subsequently visited 1st hundred, 23rd & 26th Co. A translation of some German Bde. & Regt'l Orders regarding the preparation of Trades of Work, etc., was received from 1st Div & was circulated to units. A report by Major LEWIS on the German trenches in front of FESTUBERT was submitted (with sketch) to General Staff. 1st Div's Order No 94 rec'd 9.30 p.m.	Q 497 A 223 JR 34

WAR DIARY or INTELLIGENCE SUMMARY

Army Form C. 2118.

(15)

Hour, Date, Place	Summary of Events and Information	Remarks and references to Appendices
HINGES 23-3-15 (Tuesday)	Officer with Capt. WEBBER to left of line at NEUVE CHAPELLE (previously) held by E15 Division. Coy to LOCON to see new billets there. Message rec'd from CRE. MEERUT DIVISION regarding construction of concrete plat form for 9.2" Howitzer was passed to O.C. 1st Northland Co for early action. 2 horses to R.E. Park. 2nd F. Co. moved this afternoon from GORRE to new billets at COUR ST VAAST (personnel billets) and 2 RIOUTURE (trade billets).	JR 34 JR 81 JAG-W 442 C/58 L 25- RE 72 RE 74 RE 73 L 12 RE 125 G JR 3 JR 4 19.5 RE 112 C/61 201 JR 1 JR 8
24-3-15	CRE to R.3.2 & Indland Fd. Co. Visited 2nd & 3rd Bde. HQ's & met with Brigadier of 3rd Bde. to DULUNDUR Bde. HQ to where he went O.C. 2nd F. Coy. CRE returned to HINGES 4.30 p.m. On account of the movement of troops now in progress no lorries are available today (on to-morrow) for transport of stores from R.E. Park.	JR 14 JR 13 JR 15 JR 17 RE 115 JR 12 RE 45 Q 506 G 455

Army Form C. 2118.

WAR DIARY
or
INTELLIGENCE SUMMARY.
(Erase heading not required.)

Instructions regarding War Diaries and Intelligence Summaries are contained in F.S. Regs., Part II. and the Staff Manual respectively. Title pages will be prepared in manuscript.

(16)

Hour, Date, Place	Summary of Events and Information	Remarks and references to Appendices
HINGES 25-3-15 (Thursday)	No lorries to-day Pt D.E. Headquarters left HINGES 10.35 a.m. & proceeded to new billets at LOCON, arriving 11.45 a.m. Good accommodation was obtained for Officers & horses, but the men's billets were shocking and filthy. 4 hr. " RUSE, 2.6/D Fd Co. was inspected this evening whilst working at new front line trenches. Pt Dur M 1343 r c'd - Question re: shelters to w/p can carry & send from Rotin.	JR 23 JR 64 ZA 13
LOCON 26-3-15	CRE. to 2.6/15 Co. and worked defences at CRESCENT, strongpoints visited 3rd Bde HQ 4 lorries to BERGUETTE. Lieut. LEEMING reported his arrival at 10.50 a.m. with a party of 3 specially enlisted tunnellers & 11 men transferred from 9 & 2 Regts. This party had come up fr. HAVRE under instructions from Major NORTON GRIFFITHS to join 170th Co. R.E. The party marched off at 3.30 p.m. & proceeded to 2.6/15 Co. to join N° 2 Tunnelling Section 170th Co. R.E.	MB 3 G 498 SC 100 RE 135 (X) JR 35 230 2/63 (Y)

(73989) W4141—463. 400,000. 9/14. H.&J.Ltd. Forms/C. 2118/10.

Army Form C. 2118.

WAR DIARY
or
INTELLIGENCE SUMMARY.
(Erase heading not required.)

Instructions regarding War Diaries and Intelligence Summaries are contained in F.S. Regs., Part II. and the Staff Manual respectively. Title pages will be prepared in manuscript.

(17)

Hour, Date, Place	Summary of Events and Information	Remarks and references to Appendices
LOCON 26-3-15 (contd.)	thus 1st Divs A message was recd from 1st Corps directing that Corpl. PREEDY should take up the duties of O.C. 170th Mining Co. This message was telephoned on by Adjt. to 2nd D.E. at 10.55 p.m. & the message from him returned to 1st Divn next morning, stating action taken.	
27-3-15	CRE. to 1st, 2nd & 3rd Bde HQ's — to collect offrs for commanding 2 Mining Companies (1st Divn N° 1246) CRE's report (a copy of which is filed with the "Mines papers") was sent back to 1st Division at 5.30 p.m. 1st Corps N° 252 (k) recd — Mine-regulns to be kept & weekly reports to be submitted. 1st Divn N° 1246/5 recd. CRE visited all three Field Companies. 6.20 p— Drawing of Post made by 2/Lt Duncan at BREWERY, NEUVE CHAPELLE, received from CRE 8th Division. 2/Lt Morris returned to HQ. of 1st Signal Co. RE.	JR 4 JR 3 JR 5 RE 2 RE 52R (A) R01 RE 7F JR 7 JR 6 RN 94 236 c. 21 (B) RE 124 JR 11

WAR DIARY
or
INTELLIGENCE SUMMARY.
(Erase heading not required.)

Army Form C. 2118.

Instructions regarding War Diaries and Intelligence Summaries are contained in F. S. Regs., Part II. and the Staff Manual respectively. Title pages will be prepared in manuscript.

Hour, Date, Place	Summary of Events and Information	Remarks and references to Appendices
28.3.15 LOCON	LEWIS CRE (with Major ~~Lewis~~) visited supporting points (a new line of defence) in rear of NEUVE CHAPELLE. Met G. O.C. of 3rd Bd. H.Q. (who soon after this time is) and noted the matter. Major WEEKES visited 2/3rd Howitzer Fd. Bty. Search light in process of 2/3rd Fd. Cl. was handed over to 2/3 D.F. at BETHUNE who is in [?] of Coys. Fine, N. cold wind. Lieut. SEABROOKE 2/6 C.E. returned from leave. On men 26th G. [?] was wounded.	
29.3.15 LOCON	Capt RICHARDSON handed in duty of at Capt Bonsey to Major ~~WEEKES~~ Capt RICHARDSON his unit (26/07) CRE & Major WEEKES visited 2/3 + Zealand Cy. & after CRE visited with G. O.C. to ~~artillery~~ LACOUTURE + return to 3rd Bd. H.Q. Fine & cold wind.	
30.3.15 LOCON	CRE inspected G.O.C. round trenches at NEUVE CHAPELLE, Major WEEKES visited all three C.P.s to ascertain actual requirements. and progress of work. Major ADDISON visited 1st Div. in morning to discuss reorganisation of mining units. Instruct recd Hd. Offrs. Brighton. Lieut RUSE (wounded) will join on 31st inst. returns from Op. Routine after ascend. Fine, very cold wind.	

Army Form C. 2118.

WAR DIARY
or
INTELLIGENCE SUMMARY.
(Erase heading not required.)

Instructions regarding War Diaries and Intelligence Summaries are contained in F.S. Regs., Part II. and the Staff Manual respectively. Title pages will be prepared in manuscript.

Hour, Date, Place	Summary of Events and Information	Remarks and references to Appendices
31.3.15 LOCON	Fine, warm. CRE with Capt BOYD, R.E., to NEUVE CHAPPELLE. Country greatly imroved with supporting position. 2nd A&D EDWARDS, R.E. arrived in relief of 2nd RUSS. Applicate submitted for his the photo to 25°67. and for 2nd SETRBROOKE Survai in 26°C, 16 which he has for some time attacked. Mining stores being carried up to GR 25°3 and 26°C,7 R.E. Park carried supply of wire, lit will take certain. two trains arrived for tactical officers this from here to the clearup in light trains (in's hand) in both 2d WELSH Ry.	R 15 11. 274. A Wendom Bry m. L CRE 1st Ges 2.4.15.

(73989) W4141—463. 400,000. 9/14. H.&J.Ltd. Forms/C. 2118/10.

H.Q. 1st Div. Engineers
121/5238
NO. 9
Army Form C. 2118.
April 1915

WAR DIARY
or
INTELLIGENCE SUMMARY.
(Erase heading not required.)

Hour, Date, Place	Summary of Events and Information	Remarks and references to Appendices
1.4.15 LOCON	Fine, warm, cloudless. CRE to NEUVE CHAPELLE with Major LEWIS, to discuss provision of shelters and arrange for a head line in trenches to the Maur road 23 + Loweand G2d. Major WEEKES inspected road in Div. area, the maintenance of which falls on Tr. O.E. in accordance with instructions recently received. Lt Col HARVEY OSO came over O.E. CRE arranged situation with a Major in HOUSE 4. Lu'd of 2nd Div. Am. as 2nd Div. Am. not prepared yet to carry on with it. Major MORTON and Capt. PREZD' arrived to discuss command of No. Trinity Coy. They will be 23rd + 26th Coys with Major WEEKES. Two platoons to march B.C. 170 (?) being employed for Fd. Coy, digging drains at Sq. 23b + 26b G1 to provide greater shelter to the huts noted to their West. Coys being emp. instructed G.E. 170 & Coys into work in land covered with his m autotility. I hope every br. officer will work out to assist in general of above.	Work points for April attached.
1 Div to 112 1/2.
E 110

Army Form C. 2118.

WAR DIARY
or
INTELLIGENCE SUMMARY.
(Erase heading not required.)

Instructions regarding War Diaries and Intelligence Summaries are contained in F.S. Regs., Part II. and the Staff Manual respectively. Title pages will be prepared in manuscript.

Hour, Date, Place	Summary of Events and Information	Remarks and references to Appendices
2.4.15 LOCON	CRE and Maj WEEKES to LOUVAND & about from down & fields and alerts from RE back to Fy. Lt. as hind the changed from us to cut for the mot equip't wants, others to steer in wheel signed by CRE and to issue to thingeel. Sanitary instruction issued to OP. Fine day. 2nd DD MATTHEW joined 23rd (1st F. hosp) 6.170.G1	1st Div. 1241 1st Army RE 132
3.4.15 LOCON	CRE to 26.G1. in morning. Map WEEKES to BETHUNE to purchase timber; Reg'd 500 baulks of 9"×3" and 500 metres of 6"×2". Photo of Bn. Staff 1pm. In afternoon CRE & Maj WEEKES held 3rd B.H.Q. but G.O.C. 1st Br. there Discussed details in con- nection with defence of NEUVE CHAPPELLE. Lieut CALTHROP slightly wounded (bullet) when we eye.	

WAR DIARY
or
INTELLIGENCE SUMMARY.
(Erase heading not required.)

Army Form C. 2118.

Hour, Date, Place	Summary of Events and Information	Remarks and references to Appendices
4.4.15 LOCON	CRE and Major WEEKES visited trenches in RUE DU BOIS section of defence with O.C. 23rd Bn in return marked H.Q. of B.P. Found communicating trench 6 P.S. 47 incomplete. Rainy in morning. Fine later.	W.35 E.122 E.123
5.4.15 LOCON	Drizzly Rain. Warm. CRE visited NEUVE CHAPELLE. Major WEEKES to MERVILLE where he inspected 1000 running metres of poplar planks 9"×1½" and 1000 of 15"×3".	
6.4.15 LOCON	Fine, warm in morning, cold afternoon. CRE and Major WEEKES visited 26, 61 and 38 Bdes H.Q. to discuss various details as regards work of infantry in improving trenches and new work.	
7.4.15 LOCON	Fine, windy. CRE went with G.O.C. 1st Div. to inspect various defensive points to be held as second line. CRE afterwards visited all three companies. Lieut. LLOYD, R.P.M.C. attd to 3rd C Engineers joined. 8 days leave from 8.4.15	

Army Form C. 2118.

WAR DIARY
or
INTELLIGENCE SUMMARY.
(Erase heading not required.)

Instructions regarding War Diaries and Intelligence Summaries are contained in F.S. Regs., Part II. and the Staff Manual respectively. Title pages will be prepared in manuscript.

Hour, Date, Place	Summary of Events and Information	Remarks and references to Appendices
8.4.15, LOCON	Additional cable section arrived fr. 1st Signal Co. R.E. Strength 1 Officer and 22 other ranks. Verbal intimation was recd for 1 Coys Pack. 1 Officer and about 30 other ranks of the HHYP. STAFF FORTRESS Engineers had arrived on 8.4.15. in order to improve roads in Divisional area. Arranged to billet them in both billets of 26 C.T. Fine, cold wind. One slightly wounded, while at NEUVE CHAPELLE, by piece of shell which cut his right temple. Medical Officer hopes he will be well in 3 or 4 days. Casualty report to him sent.	
2.40 p	Lieut C.E. SHERWIN and 44 other ranks HHMP-STAFF FORTRESS Eng. arrived abt 2.30 pm. They bvyll with this Company. 1 Frep Cart, 1 G.S. wagon Maj. WEEKES went to BETHUNE and requisitioned 450 yds of 3" x 3" (battens for making) Bridges, fr. M. OUTREBON, Staff has both seen upon despatch to 23.3.67.	W 37

Army Form C. 2118.

WAR DIARY
or
INTELLIGENCE SUMMARY.
(Erase heading not required.)

Hour, Date, Place	Summary of Events and Information	Remarks and references to Appendices
9.4.15 LOCON	HAMPSHIRE Engineers refused to commence improving QUEEN MARY ROAD tomorrow LOWLAND C² refused to take over work in sect. D2 of line, as far as and including 2nd S Bde, from 2nd 23° C¹.	W.35
	Ad. CRE (Major WEEKES) visited all three companies. Proposed by Lt. Col. 178th Coy. Brit.Div. 2nd 2 Feb. 170 C¹ from 1st Div. and transp. them to 23° Div as there is no work for them in NEUVE CHAPELLE sector. 23° and 26 C¹ refused to send upon tomorrow desire to cart metal for HAMPSHIRE Engineers from a ruined 1st Div. kiln to 77 Sd 9.4.15 finish. — Het sht. of E 3 cuts on front of D3 sects is to be headed on to MEERUT Div — n 11 and 12. 2nd B.E. Engrs break new H NGES. 26 C¹ billets heavily shelled in afternoon — to work.	W.38 J.R.S
Saturday 10.4.15 LOCON.	Fine Day. A/CRE to RUE Du BOIS with Br. 23° C¹ ordered out for day out. Them to 23 1st H.Q. tonight. all 3 C.E.	

Army Form C. 2118.

WAR DIARY
or
INTELLIGENCE SUMMARY.
(Erase heading not required.)

Instructions regarding War Diaries and Intelligence Summaries are contained in F.S. Regs., Part II. and the Staff Manual respectively. Title pages will be prepared in manuscript.

Hour, Date, Place	Summary of Events and Information	Remarks and references to Appendices
11.4.15. LOCON	Arranged that 26 G.I should all remain in back billets when men of 23rd take place. Any employ'ts in new S. & M. billets near RICHEBOURG 23rd HOWLAND G.T.G remain in front billets. 26 G.I moved billets you shelled in afternoon. A/CRE visited DI Snt. with Maj. ARTHUR. also in front ridges. Division informed regarding his views. Then visited 23rd G.I. Lovely day. Sent R.M. TOBIN the proof of 170. G.T RE & M. Div. decided to attach him to his 2 Sct. 2Lt HTF. G. ROUSE (Royal Field Art. Eng. "J") posted to No 1 Sct 170 G.I via 2 Zeal. DARLINGTON, 4 WELSH. Fusiliers who regains his unit tonight. Major C. RUSSELL BROWN recommended for [?] staff appointment.	1st Corps A.O.S 7 1st Corps A.O.S 4 E 116 E 123
12.4.15 LOCON	Fine day. CRE returning to duty troops. M 13th HQ. with GOR 1st Div. Then 15. 23rd & 26 to CO LATVO GR JULLUNDER 1st proposed bridge 26 G.I G.T.G men left LOBES. Maj. WEEKES visited them at [?]	

Army Form C. 2118.

WAR DIARY
or
INTELLIGENCE SUMMARY.
(Erase heading not required.)

Instructions regarding War Diaries and Intelligence Summaries are contained in F.S. Regs., Part II and the Staff Manual respectively. Title pages will be prepared in manuscript.

170/30

Hour, Date, Place	Summary of Events and Information	Remarks and references to Appendices
13-4-15 LOCON.	Found Mr Loo wall and inventory, 1st Sus [sic] 2nd METRNT Div objects to man unless good billets can be found for 26 Coy. L aft in Hqs WEEKES visits 26 Coy and saw with work. 26 Coy billets again shelled today. Decided to return to Hqts 2 Sect. 170 Coy with 26 Coy and start new mine in 83. 2nd Lieut to 170 Coy and Lieut HOPPS PS H.Q.R.E. Further engineer work D.O.O. S.th. billets near RICHE- BOURG to look into for 26 Coy to have broken billets tomorrow. C.R.E visited RUE de BOIS Section (W₂) with Capt BOYD G.S. and Major ARTHUR and new visited Lowland Field Coy. Temp Lieut H.F.G. ROOSE joined No 1 Section 170 N Coy R.E. (attached to 23rd Fd Coy RE) C.R.E went on leave to England till 23rd inst and instructs Major WEEKES to act	

Army Form C. 2118.

WAR DIARY
or
INTELLIGENCE SUMMARY.
(Erase heading not required.)

Hour, Date, Place	Summary of Events and Information	Remarks and references to Appendices
14.4.15. LOCON	Lieut. E.E. CALTHROP R.E. ordered in to act as adjutant with effect from 14.4.15.	W.57
	Cold and showery.	
	C.R.E. visits 23rd, 26th, and LOWLAND Field Coys in the morning.	
	Lt. CALTHROP arrived to act as adjutant.	
	In the afternoon the C.R.E. visits Hdq. 1st Divn. to confer with G.O.C. 1st Div.	
	Lieut. B.M. TORIN. R.E. joined No. 2 Section 170R Coy. R.E. (att'd 26th Fd Coy. R.E.)	
	Temp'd Lieut E.C. DANIELS. R.E. joined No. 1 Section. 170R Coy. R.E. (att'd 23rd Fd Coy R.E.)	

Army Form C. 2118.

WAR DIARY
or
INTELLIGENCE SUMMARY.
(Erase heading not required.)

Instructions regarding War Diaries and Intelligence Summaries are contained in F.S. Regs., Part II. and the Staff Manual respectively. Title pages will be prepared in manuscript.

Hour, Date, Place	Summary of Events and Information	Remarks and references to Appendices
15.4.15 LOCON	Fine day. Sunny. In morning C.R.E. went to select a site near HINGES for construction of entrenchments for practice purposes - hence to see amount of road metal available. He then visited 23rd Lowland Fd Coys at LE TOURET and 26th Fd Coy at LA COUTURE, inspecting repairs to QUEEN MARYS & KING GEORGES roads. C.R.E. then to took Major LEWIS R.E. to HINGES position - (practice breastworks). Ad/adj went into BETHUNE and tennis (none). 220 lengths of 6"x2½" from M. OUTREBON arrangements made for one batt^n from 2nd B^de to be put under C.R.E's control for work.	
16.4.15 LOCON	Fine day. C.R.E. and Adjutant, with Major Russell Brown & Major Arthur for shelter behind the houses on N side of RUE OUBLOIS and back along second line breastworks.	

WAR DIARY
or
INTELLIGENCE SUMMARY.
(Erase heading not required.)

Army Form C. 2118.

Hour, Date, Place	Summary of Events and Information	Remarks and references to Appendices
	In afternoon C.R.E. and adjutant visited work which was being commenced near HINGES. C.R.E. then visited Hqrs. 3rd Bde. 23rd F.Coy. Lowland Fd Coy and 26th Fd Coy. He then went to RICHEBOURG to see O.C. Loyal North Lancs — Re Battn details) to work under C.R.E. 1 Draughtsman R.E. arrived & posted to 26th Coy.	G.580
17.4.15. LOCON.	Fine day. C.R.E. accompanied by adjt. visit Lowland Fd Coy and inspect horses and billets. Then to 23rd Fd Coy. C.R.E. inspects work being done on roads in X.15 (36 a b c map). C.R.E. then visits O.C. Loyal North Lancs and arranges organisation of working parties. Colonel GODBY. C.E. as Major ADDISON visit Hqrs. 1st D.E. in morning. Col. SCHOFIELD C.R.E. 2nd D.W. visits Hqrs. 1st D.E. in evening. 2nd Lieut ROOSE R.E. joins No.1 Sectn. 170th Coy R.E.	

Army Form C. 2118.

WAR DIARY
or
INTELLIGENCE SUMMARY.
(Erase heading not required.)

Hour, Date, Place	Summary of Events and Information	Remarks and references to Appendices
18.4.15 LOCON	Fine day. C.R.E. informed that LOYAL NORTH LANCS are to be withdrawn from RICHEBOURG on 19R. C.R.E. visits 3rd Bde H.Qr. and arranges for a battalion to take their place. — Then visits 23rd and Lowland Field companies. Adjr. collects lists of stores in hand from 23rd 26R and Lowland Fd Cos. In afternoon C.R.E. and adj. visit and inspect breastwork (for practice) at VERTBOIS farm near HINGES.	
19.4.15 LOCON	Morning. C.R.E. goes round RUE de Bois position with Major ARTHUR and then visits 23rd & LOWLAND Field Coys. — then visits 26R Fd Coy RE adj. goes into HINGES to arrange for supply of Timber (4½"×3" and 9" planking)	

WAR DIARY
or
INTELLIGENCE SUMMARY.
(Erase heading not required.)

Army Form C. 2118.

Instructions regarding War Diaries and Intelligence Summaries are contained in F.S. Regs., Part II. and the Staff Manual respectively. Title pages will be prepared in manuscript.

Hour, Date, Place	Summary of Events and Information	Remarks and references to Appendices
20.4.15 LOCON	In evening. C.R.E. attends conference at 1st Div. H.Q. C.R.E. assisted, accompanied by ADS inspects line of breastwork running E from ALBERT road to point S8d 9/6 and now inspect ALBERT Rd & RUE du BERCEAUX and Tracks running from here to find most suitable way of carrying up R.E. stores to RUE de BOIS. C.R.E. then visits Lowland & 23rd Field Coys. 2nd Lieut 170th Coy. R.E. (att'd 23 Coy) reports as having been withdrawn from 1st Div area. 170th Coy. R.E. from arrival of 43 miners for 1st Guards Brigade reported.	

Army Form C. 2118.

WAR DIARY
or
INTELLIGENCE SUMMARY.
(Erase heading not required.)

Instructions regarding War Diaries and Intelligence Summaries are contained in F.S. Regs., Part II. and the Staff Manual respectively. Title pages will be prepared in manuscript.

Hour, Date, Place	Summary of Events and Information	Remarks and references to Appendices
21.4.15 LOCON.	C.E. visits Hq. 1st D.E. and then goes with CRE and adj. to 26th Coy. RE at LA COUTURE. CRE and adj. then visit 23rd and Lowland Fd Coys. Two sections of 26th Field Coy. detailed to work one with 23rd Fd Coy. the other with Lowland Fd Coy. Temporarily. Colonel Schreiber returns to duty.	W.63. of 20.4.15
22.4.15 LOCON.	Fine day. C.E. visits RUE DE BOIS Section of Line with Major Russell Brown C.R.E. and adjt. visited all the Companies No 1 Mining Section 170th Coy RE ordered to leave the division by 1st Army on Transfer to 2nd Division, there leaving 1st Division without miners. Lt. E.E. Callthrop returned to 26th Field Coy RE on completion of duty as acting adjutant which Major Weekes resumed with effect from this date.	Q.195

(73989) W4141—463. 400,000. 9/14. H.&J. Ltd. Forms/C. 2118/10.

WAR DIARY
or
INTELLIGENCE SUMMARY.
(Erase heading not required.)

Army Form C. 2118.

Hour, Date, Place	Summary of Events and Information	Remarks and references to Appendices
23.4.15 LOCON	Fine day. C.R.E. and Adjt. visited RUE du Bois and inspected lines C. & D. with O.C. 23rd F.d Coy and O.C. Lowland F.d Coy. and were shelled while there and on the way back. Arrangements made for special issue of 50000 sandbags for Depôts, and daily issue of 12000. Arrangements made for extra supply of hurdles from LAPUGNOY. Transport by motor lorries arranged with the Supply Column.	CES No. 31 &c
24.4.15 LOCON	Fine day. Orders received to move LOWLAND Coy billet by 3p.m. today, in order to accommodate 2nd London Field Coy here. C.R.E. visited Lowland Coy about accommodation and then went to Div. H.Q. Above order cancelled owing to loss of time involved and difficulty of transporting stores. In afternoon C.R.E. and Adjt. visited all the Coys.	

WAR DIARY
or
INTELLIGENCE SUMMARY.
(Erase heading not required.)

Army Form C. 2118.

Hour, Date, Place	Summary of Events and Information	Remarks and references to Appendices
25.4.15. LOCON.	C.R.E. visited all the Coys in the morning. Major Weekes ordered to take over 2nd line work under C.R.E. MEERUT Division and left for STEEBECQUE. Lieut E.E. Calthrop ordered to rejoin as acting adjutant and reports at 12 noon	E.135
26.4.15 LOCON.	C.R.E. inspects work on Section D2. RUE de Bois Line with O.C. Lowland Field Coy and on return visits G.O.C. 2nd Bde. Adjr. attends practice of attack war braziwaks at VERTBOIS Farm and arranges for supply of material for experiments in getting Field Guns over small dykes. Lecture by G.O.C. 1st Div on the "attack" at LOCON in the evening	E.137

Army Form C. 2118.

WAR DIARY
or
INTELLIGENCE SUMMARY.
(Erase heading not required.)

Instructions regarding War Diaries and Intelligence Summaries are contained in F.S. Regs., Part II. and the Staff Manual respectively. Title pages will be prepared in manuscript.

Hour, Date, Place	Summary of Events and Information	Remarks and references to Appendices
27.4.15. LOCON.	Fine day. Cloudy in afternoon. CRE visits 23rd & Lowland Field Coy in the morning. In evening CRE had conference with GOC 3rd Bde. Adj. visits 23rd 26th & Lowland F.Coys to arrange about collection storing and making up of hand grenades for each brigade.	
28.4.15 LOCON.	Fine day C.R.E goes round C. and D. Lines of Section D.3. RUE du BOIS with Major Russell Brown and recce visits 23rd & Lowland Field Coy Billets 1st Div Pontoons received from 2nd Div. Arra.	Ca. 4.

Army Form C. 2118.

WAR DIARY
or
INTELLIGENCE SUMMARY.
(Erase heading not required.)

Hour, Date, Place	Summary of Events and Information	Remarks and references to Appendices
29.4.15. LOCON.	CRE. goes round C. & D. lines of D.3. Section with Major Russell Brown and then visits 23rd Lowland and 26th Field Coy RE. CRE. granted sick leave from 30th Inst. and Major Russell Brown is ordered to take over duties as acting CRE. and reports at H.Q at 4 p.m. CRE. and Major Russell Brown attend Conference at Div. H.Q.	
30.4.15. LOCON.	Colonel Schreiber goes on sick leave for 8 days and Major Russell Brown takes over duties with effect from this date. a/ CRE. visits 83rd & Lowland Fd Coys RE. to discuss programme of work. adj. visits 26th Coy. RE. to discuss construction of scaling ladders and river bridges.	

"A" Form. Army Form C. 2121.
MESSAGES AND SIGNALS. No. of Message..........

Prefix....... Code...... m.	Words	Charge	This message is on a/c of:	Recd. at........m.
Office of Origin and Service Instructions	Sent		............Service.	Date............
....	At..........m.			From............
....	To............			
....	By............		(Signature of "Franking Officer.")	By............

| TO | O.C. 26 C/7 | | |
| | | | |

| Sender's Number. | Day of Month. | In reply to Number | AAA |
| W 35 | 8.4.15 | | |

(1). Strength of Det. Hampshire Fortress Engineers which arrives this afternoon is 1 officer, 2 Sergeants, 33 other ranks, 1 N.C.O + 3 drivers, 9 horses, 1 forge cart, 1 G.S. wagon.

(2) They should commence work tomorrow in improving QUEEN MARY Road, starting from road junction at second U of LACOUTURE (R 35 d), working towards RICHEBOURG.

H. B. Smith
Major

From	1 D.E.			
Place				
Time				

The above may be forwarded as now corrected. (Z)
....
Censor. Signature of Addressor or person authorised to telegraph in his name.
* This line should be erased if not required.

"A" Form.
Army Form C. 2121.

MESSAGES AND SIGNALS.

Prefix	Code	m.	Words	Charge	* This message is on a/c of:	Recd. at	m.
Office of Origin and Service Instructions			Sent		Service.	Date	
			At	m.		From	
			To			By	
			By		(Signature of "Franking Officer.")		

| TO | 26" Field Ary | | | |

| Sender's Number. | Day of Month. | In reply to Number | AAA |
| E.116 | 11-4 | | |

Your unit will move to new
billets on morning of 13th
and continue march to tit there

From CMR
Place
Time 10 50 am

The above may be forwarded as now corrected. (Z)

Censor.   Signature of Addressor or person authorised to telegraph in his name.

* This line should be erased if not required.

"A" Form. Army Form C. 2121.

MESSAGES AND SIGNALS.

TO 23rd Field Coy.

Sender's Number: E108
Day of Month: 11-4

Lieut Darlington will rejoin his Battalion today aaa His Battalion wants to keep his baggage.

From: 1st D.L.I.
Time: 11 am

"C" Form (Duplicate). Army Form C. 2123.

MESSAGES AND SIGNALS.

No. of Message

SM DH 7 ACO Batchelor

Charges to Pay. £ 2

Service Instructions.

Handed in at 5H Bde Office 4-40 m. Received 8 m.

TO **CRE 1st Div**

Sender's Number	Day of Month	In reply to Number	AAA
170/30	13		

2nd Lieut Roose RE arrived 10 am today

report to CO

FROM PLACE & TIME: 170th C RE

"A" Form.   Army Form C. 2121.

MESSAGES AND SIGNALS.   No. of Message _____

Office... m. and Service Instructions	Words	Charge	This message is on a/c of: _____ Service. (Signature of "Franking Officer.")	Recd. at _____ m. Date _____ From _____ By _____
	Sent At _____ m. To _____ By _____			

TO { Oc 26 G7

Sender's Number.	Day of Month.	In reply to Number	A A A
W S7	13.4.15		

Send	List	CALTHROP	to	H.Q
early	tomorrow	to	ask	as
as				

From 1st DE

Place

Time

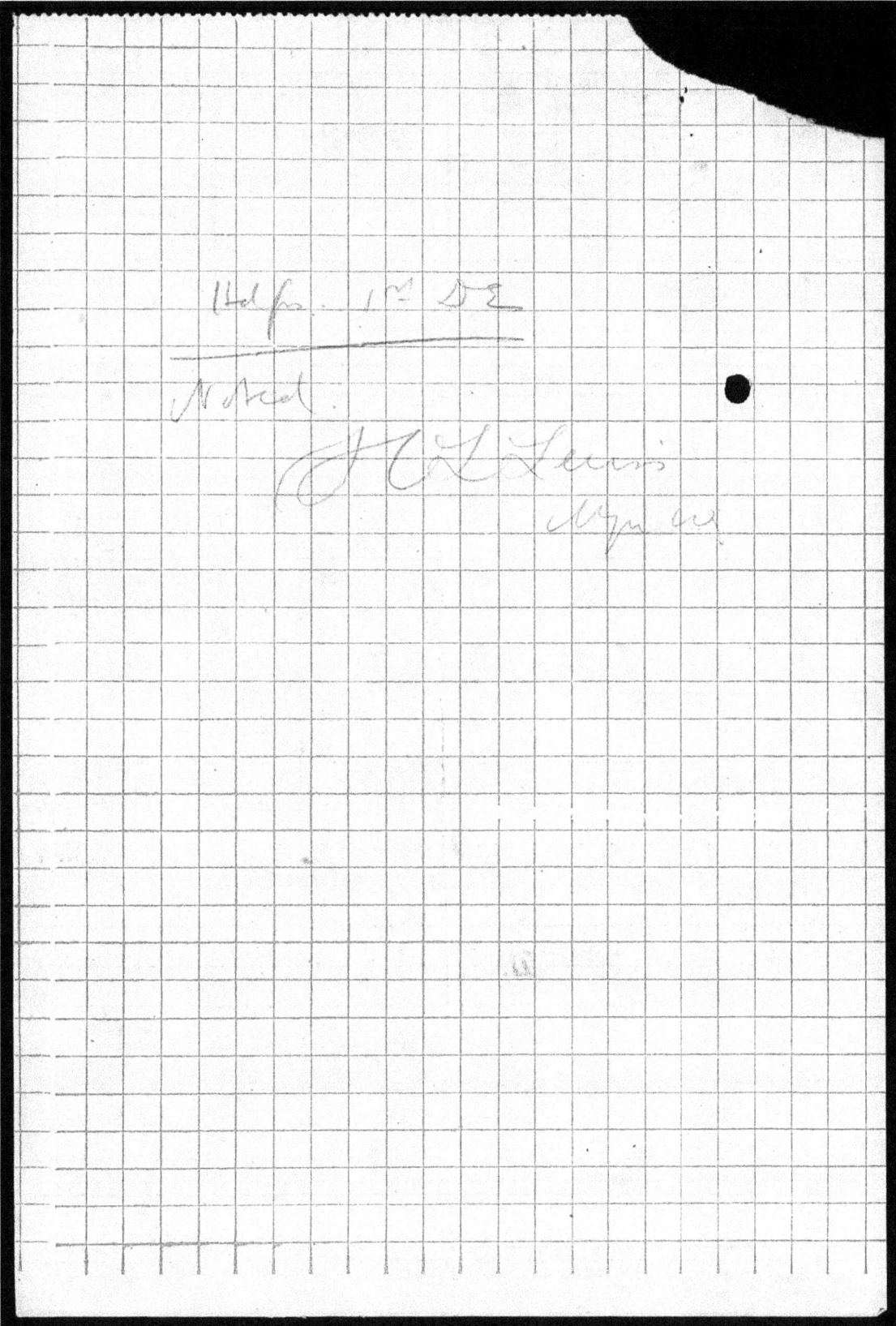

"A" Form. — MESSAGES AND SIGNALS. — Army Form C. 2121.

TO: CRE 1 Div

Sender's Number: 31 **Day of Month:** 23.4.15 **AAA**

1st Corps is sending 8 lorries to Le Touret with railway on Saturday Sunday + Monday AAA arriving at 8.30 a.m. AAA arrange for working parties to unload near Le Touret + manhandle at night to depot screened from aerial

"A" Form. Army Form C. 2121.
MESSAGES AND SIGNALS.

Observation to be selected by you vice S 14a Rue de Bois AAA site selected yesterday not available AAA report position chosen

From CE 1 Corps

C Godley

...GES AND SIGNALS.

TO: OC Det. HAMPSHIRE Engineers

Sender's Number: W 7... Day of Month: 23.4.15 AAA

Eight lorries of light railway material are arriving at LE TOURET by lorry at 8.30a on Saturday Sunday Monday AAA. Arrange to meet them and unload them then on site convert to 20 67 AAA Convoy them after dark to S.14.A.5.2 AAA Place at and Store them then AAA Actual place selected must be screened from aerial observation

Time: 4p

"A" Form.   Army Form C. 2121.

MESSAGES AND SIGNALS.

No. of Message _____

Prefix	Code	m.	Words	Charge	This message is on a/c of:	Recd. at ____ m.
Office of Origin and Service Instructions.			Sent			Date
			At ____ m.		____ Service.	From
			To			By
			By		(Signature of "Franking Officer.")	

TO   CRE 1st Div

Sender's Number: 22   Day of Month: In reply to Number: **AAA**

Please direct Havre ½ to RE with you to select depots for wood railway to unload transport there it arrive B or 4 days and later to lay same.

From: CE
Place:
Time:

Censor: Godby

O.C. Hampshire Fort. Engineer

(1) This railway (2 miles long) is being made in the Bomb factory, and some of it will be ready in a few days. Please ascertain [?] for Lt Bateman when he will [be for despatch?]

(2) It [should] be unloaded at

MESSAGES AND SIGNALS.

"A" Form.   Army Form C. 2121.

TO 26th Field Coy.

Sender's Number.	Day of Month.	In reply to Number	
E.175.	25.4		A A A

Regret that owing to Major Walker being ordered away must call on Company in for services of Lieut. Col Thrupp also. He must report here before 12 noon today

From OMS
Place
Time 7 am

"A" Form. Army Form C. 2121.
MESSAGES AND SIGNALS.

TO: 1st D.E.

Sender's Number: G580
Day of Month: 16/4

Second one Battalion RICHEBOURG St AM. Billets by will be Inf Bde 17th inclusive furnish working by C.R.E. be available

Inf Battalion to VAAST Billets will be Inf Bde attached for 17 inclusive AAA working parties C.R.E. and available for

Bde to VAAST will be Bde AAA attached to supplies Battalion as will others

will proceed this will be Bde AAA to supplies Battalion will others

detail to afternoon arranged Battn 3rd from will not work ex

Addressed 2nd Inf Bde
Repeated D.E. and 3rd Inf Bde.

From: 1st Div.
Place:
Time: 9.30 am

E.H.M.

"A" Form.
MESSAGES AND SIGNALS.
Army Form C. 2121.

Prefix........ Code........ m.	Words	Charge	This message is on a/c of:	Recd. at........ m.
Office of Origin and Service Instructions	Sent			Date........
	At........ m.		........Service.	From........
	To........		(Signature of "Franking Officer.")	By........
	By........			

TO { Headquarters 1st C.E.

| Sender's Number. | Day of Month. | In reply to Number | AAA |
| JR | 9-4-15 | | |

Lieutenant C.E. SHERWIN and 44 other ranks of the 1st 2nd HANTS (Fortress) Co RE (T) reported here this afternoon & have been accommodated in back billets. Your instructions regarding work on roads have been communicated to this officer.

J W Richard Capt. RE

From 1st Co. RE
Place
Time

The above may be forwarded as now corrected. (Z)

Censor. Signature of Addressor or person authorised to telegraph in his name.
* This line should be erased if not required.

"A" Form.
MESSAGES AND SIGNALS.
Army Form C. 2121.

TO	G.H.Q.

Sender's Number	Day of Month	In reply to Number	
W97	8.4.15		AAA

Colonel ACTON L. SCHREIBER D.S.O. ADC slightly wounded

From: 1st DIV
Place: 3.40 am

"A" Form.   Army Form C. 2121.
MESSAGES AND SIGNALS.   No. of Message_____

Prefix___ Code___ m.	Words	Charge	This message is on a/c of:	Recd. at___ m.
Office of Origin and Service Instructions_				Date___
	Sent		___Service.	From___
___	At___ m			
___	To___		___	By___
	By___		(Signature of "Franking Officer.")	

| TO | O.C. 26th Coy R.E. | | | |

| Sender's Number. | Day of Month. | In reply to Number | AAA |
| Y 30 | 7-4-15. | | |

One	officer	and	about	30
other	ranks	Hampshire	Regt.	will
arrive	at your	back	billets	some
time	evening	of	eighth	April.
A.A.A.	Arrange	billets	and	rations
for	ninth.	AAA	They	are
for	work	on	roads	

(Sd) H.W. Weekes
From P.D.C.
Major R.E.
Place
Time

MESSAGES AND SIGNALS. Army Form C. 2121.

No. of Message _____

Prefix _____ Code _____ m. | Words | Charge | This message is on a/c of: | Recd. at _____ m.
Office of Origin and Service Instructions | | | | Date _____
_____ | Sent | | _____ Service. | From _____
_____ | At _____ m. | | (Signature of "Franking Officer.") | By _____
_____ | To _____ | | |
_____ | By _____ | | |

TO {
_____
_____
_____
}

* Sender's Number | Day of Month | In reply to Number | AAA

...... in conjunction with the
...... shown ......
......
......
......
......
an Officer should attend.

A. L. Schreiber
Colonel.

From 1st D.E.
Place _____
Time 6.30 p.m.

The above may be forwarded as now corrected.   (Z)

Censor. | Signature of Addressor or person authorised to telegraph in his name.

* This line should be erased if not required.

MESSAGES AND SIGNALS.

"A" Form.   Army Form C. 2121.

TO: 26th Fd Coy.   Pressing

Sender's Number: E.177   Day of Month: 25   AAA

The G.O.C. in C. 1st Army will inspect practice operations at VERTBOIS Fm tomorrow (26) at 11 a.m. Will Please arrange that sufficient camel bridges and tree leg improvements will be made also in moving field guns over small ditches about not more than 6' wide. Please arrange for sufficient material for one bridge or ways of any material you have — not cut especially for the purpose to be on the ground. If you can possibly produce a pair of large cartwheels and axle (and lashings) to

"A" Form.
Army Form C. 2121.

MESSAGES AND SIGNALS.

No. of Message _____

Prefix _____ Code _____ m.
Office of Origin and Service Instructions.

Words | Charge

Sent
At _____ m.
To _____
By _____

This message is on a/c of :

_____ Service.

(Signature of "Franking Officer.")

Recd. at _____ m.
Date _____
From _____
By _____

TO — 1st D⟨iv⟩

Sender's Number: G195
Day of Month: 22nd.
In reply to Number:
AAA

Notification has now been received from 1st Corps that remaining section of 170th Mining Company RE will join H.Q. of Company with 2nd Division.

From 1st Div.
Place
Time 8.45 am

The above may be forwarded as now corrected.
(Z)
Censor. Signature of Addressor or person authorised to telegraph in his name.
*This line should be erased if not required.

"A" Form. Army Form C. 2121.

MESSAGES AND SIGNALS. No. of Message

Prefix	Code	m.	Words	Charge	This message is on a/c of:	Recd. at	m.
Office of Origin and Service Instructions		Sent			Service.	Date	
		At	m.			From	
		To			(Signature of "Franking Officer.")	By	
		By					

TO { 2nd Brigade

Sender's Number.	Day of Month.	In reply to Number	A A A
E192	7 H		

Reference question of finding billets for an extra Field Coy this is not now necessary as the extra company will not now be transferred to your section.

From 1st DE
Place
Time 4.30 pm

The above may be forwarded as now corrected. (Z) [signature]

"A" Form. Army Form C. 2121.

MESSAGES AND SIGNALS.

TO: 1st Brigade

Sender's Number.	Day of Month.	In reply to Number	AAA
E.123	7-4		

In view of importance of completion of front line in D.2. Westland Field Coy will remain in your sector and on proposed time it would take over Inspection D.2 as far as Butts. Do you concur.

From: CRE
Time: 5.10 pm

MESSAGES AND SIGNALS.

TO	23rd
	OC 26th Field Coy RE.
	Lowland

Sender's Number.	Day of Month.	In reply to Number	AAA
Ca 4.	27th		

The necessary bridging wagons are to be at the Barge Bridge over the canal E of GORRE by 10 a.m. They will park near and go up singly via CAMBRI as ordered by the officer there. No parties will be sent with wagons as bridging equipment will be loaded by 2nd Div.

S E Callthrop
Lt RE
a/ adj 1st D.E

1st DIVISION ENGINEERS DAILY PROGRESS REPORT.

FROM MID-DAY 30=4=15. TO MID-DAY 1=5=15.

Section.	Company.	
	26th Field Co.	2 Sections with 23rd Bty R.E. Other sections preparing material
D.3.	23rd Field Coy.	10 yds new trenchwork with Gunners commenced just north of Lane X. Work continued on Parapets on "A" line & dugouts behind Lane X. Breastworks at H.Q. D.S. Section (1) South wing, Parados revetted all along & completely either sap except for test fags – & traverses finished & the new ones commenced. (1) Junction with Parapet completely earthed up. Parados completed, revetted & earthed, (2) North work – Traverse at D1 end complete.
D.1.	1st Lowland Fd. Coy.	Repairs to King George's Rd at RICHEBOURG. Barricade at corner of Edward Rd. Rue du Bois raised & thickened. Traverses on "D"line already finished – 5 yds of D1 line completed. Work on new part to A.S.C. supply store at junction of A line & Rue St Gervais – to traverses started and 5 yds parados to the level of A line to right of "D" line to left of A line to left of Arthur Rd completed to head & parapet. 25 yds of new trenchwork on D1 line to left of Arthur Rd completed to head & parapet. Traverses made – 20 yds revetment sperm. Work on Gobetrolli parapet north of Rue du Bois continued

H.C. Alber[?]
Lieut R.E. 2/Lt
Commanding R.E. 1st Divn 1st D[?]

1.15/1915.

1st DIVISION ENGINEERS DAILY PROGRESS REPORT.

FROM MID-DAY 19-4-15. TO MID-DAY 20-4-15.

Section.	Company.	
	26th Field Co.	2 Sectors with 23rd Bay Rt. Other Sections preparing material.
D.3.	23rd Field Coy.	Continued work on "D" line in H.Q.D.3. + Augusta + Res. au 23rd. Traverses carried on to all three lines. Finishes work on WRR N of N bridge of Richam.
D.2.	1st Lowland Fd. Coy.	Repairs to King George's Rd at RICHEBOURG. Line inundated completed except 50 yds to affect all 4 + 5 firework. Line Albert Road to the old Decies Road inundation being passed to new water level aground. D line mostly complete except for hostile shell craters. Two 6'0" cubes completed and front two firework on D line 3 in 1 many built + completed at 2 percent dig, each. Rest of D line 3 in 1 many needed except the inundation at 86 yds in D line 3 formean needed. Parapet parados, dugouts, firestep - & traverses of rich current undertain Average height of 5ft for a distance of 60 x 40 m D line opening properties in view of new Rd.

20/4/1915.

Commanding [signature]
for C.R.E. 1st Division

1st DIVISION ENGINEERS DAILY PROGRESS REPORT.

FROM MID-DAY 28=4=15.   TO MID-DAY 29=4=15.

Section.	Company.	
	26th Field Co.	2 sections with 23rd Coy R.E. Other sections preparing material.
D.3.	23rd Field Coy.	Richard Road end of "B" line - Filled two small gaps in line heavy revetted & completed straight trench 10" long, North of southern hedge of Orchard between 23 H.Qrs. Revetted & completed straight trench 10" long, North of northern hedge & built 2 traverses. Put up 70 ft of hurdle revetment about half way between N+S.
D.2.	1st Lowland Fd. Coy.	Repaired & Kept Georges trench at RICHEBOURG. Completed D'Oires breastwork with traverses from Seward Rd to Orchard distance 370 yds. 6 metre hurdles & traverses in new front line "D1" Section. Two Branchem Bridle + Parapet raising 3'0 for 30 yds D1 line, 6 hurdles built & parapet raised 2'0 for 60 yds, loopholes for 60 coy. Loopholes & armoured Sloper to stop at cores of bombed shops A. 1 B.G. Armoured Lining now complete.

29/4/1915.

[signature]
Lieut. R.E. for
Commanding Roy. Engr. 1st Divn.

1st DIVISION ENGINEERS DAILY PROGRESS REPORT.

FROM MID-DAY 27/4/15. TO MID-DAY 28/4/15.

Company.	Section.	
26th Field Co.		2 Sections with 23rd Coy R.E. Other Sections preparing materials.
23rd Field Coy.	D.3.	"C" line Breastwork behind R.E. store thickened but not proof everywhere. Path made from "C" line to Rue du Bois, and over bridge. Breach in retirement made good. Gap at end of "C" line over old R.E. Store inverted & much party pick dug behind same in south 7 lines. D.line. Traverse dug across & built up in the same place into knife-edge. Traverse practically bayonet-proof. Head of "D" line trench filled in to about parapet level & boyaux back to parapet thickened.
1st Lowland Fd. Coy.	R.2.	Repairs to point E. RICHEBOURG. "D" & "E" line Breastworks west of Rue du Bois, 15 travers completed. 25 complete. Drainage & knotting power behind breastwork 200 yds from Rue au Bois complete. 60" Rubble-Revetted in "D" line breastwork. Southwork is now 4'6" high except for a 25 yds stretch in 8'0"/4'0" high. Parapet being made bullet-proof. E line parapet in some 3'4"/3'0" & has in Revetment. In the front wall covering the trend traversed at intervals with sandbag walls. About traverse traits replace by sandbag walls. Front & parallel support to strong point. Parados replaced at trench average 2 ft. Strengthening outside walls being built at R.E store nearly complete.

Portion cover at R.E. Store, 5'/20"× 6' high complete.

J. Callinhoff

for Commanding Roy Engr 1st Div. Lines.

28/4 /1915.

1st DIVISION ENGINEERS DAILY PROGRESS REPORT.

FROM MID-DAY 26=4=15. TO MID-DAY 27=4=15.

Section.	Company.		
	26th Field Co.	2 Sections with 23rd Bays R.E. Other Sections preparing material.	
D.2.	23rd Field Coy.	Rendering remainder of "P" line & North nursery traverses bomb-proof. Improved 150 yds of the trench by tightening sides and cut from B line. Completed junction new trench at present CINDER TRACK & widening Redoubt.	
D.3.	1st Lowland Fd. Coy.	Repairs to King George's Road at RIGHT-BOUND. On "D" line trenches from Cousins Rd. to Gloster Manor Corner, borders, bombproofs to traverses 90 x made bulletproof, 13 hurdles & revets & hurdles of trench revetted. Bonneveau revetted a new breastwork on "C" line, training company sent working party at quarry & building Lebinar dannis in Rue au long days finished to high left. Walking bridge erected & 1 new shifter Redoubt trenched widened & deepened.	

3 bullet proof lookouts & 3 heavy bridges made for Rue du Bois.

31 / /1915.

J.B.W..... Lieut. R.E.
Adjutant 1st Div

for Commanding

1st DIVISION ENGINEERS DAILY PROGRESS REPORT.

FROM MID-DAY 25/4/15. TO MID-DAY 26/4/15.

Company.	Section.	
26th Field Co.		2 Sections rationed boy R.E. Bridge. Other Sections preparing material.
23rd Field Co.	No. 3.	Front fence for 1 P.H. front fence 135 yds. breastwork lightning completed to 4'.6" + 115 yds. more started on Rd. was posts fitted. D. Coy. D. Coy. completely ratiod + all except 30 yds 3'.0" front built up. Communication trench 30 yds instead of bypass completed.
1st Lowland Fd. Coy.	D.2.	Continuation of work on Kline breastwork. Return effect shown to firework along which line. 100 yds to 3 ft 4 8000 yds of fire shed + sealand of cap + revetment + shown + hurdles. Return to holly Georges H.H. + S.H.H. to Shelley's Hill shown. Splinter proof shelters. Quelia in Rd. nr. Rd constant. Preparation of R.E. material.

26/4/1915. For Commanding R. Eng. 2nd Engrs 1st Div.

SUMMARY OF WORK PERFORMED BY R.E. UNITS 1st DIVISION.

From MIDDAY .... to Midday ....

Section.	Company.	Work carried out.			
I. OPERATIONS. (a).					
(b).					
(a).					
(b).					
II. INFORMATION.					
III. WORK. (a). Section "C"					
(b). Section "D"					
IV. WATER. (a). Section "C".					
(b). Section "D".					

Date ....   Rank ....

1st DIVISION ENGINEERS DAILY PROGRESS REPORT. 1st DIVISION ENGINEERS DAILY PROGRESS REPORT.

FROM MID-DAY 24=4=15. TO MID-DAY 25=4=15.

Section.	Company.	Section.	Company.
	26th Field Co.	1 Sections with 23rd Coy. R.E. Other sections preparing.	
P.3.	23rd Field Coy.	"90" Revetment finished bullet proof. 160'+ over front Aug 15 Sept. 23rd Communication Trench 204'w of bpts 50' revetted both sides of 1000 Bulletproof 60' of trench which was already revetted made bullet proof.	
P.2.	1st Lowland Fd. Coy.	On "D" line bivouacs, latrines along M.T. light reserve borne to Cavan Road — Average half M.T.30, redone 35 lg M. 8 yards 30 hurdles & complete 1st Lot. cartwork & 6 lag R. Road prep. Thence off Haverin. Reconnaissance made of bridges & rails in P.2 Leat Cow Farm Artillery observation compound. Repair to King George Road, & section of [?] continued, repairs [?] [?] Richmond Observation Station. Two Canoes 4% complete [?] Cavan Rd. [?] 11/2 [?] [?] [?]	

25/4/1915.

20th ? 10 ? ?
SS ? 31 ? ?
[signature]
1/1915. Commanding Lieut R.E. for
2040 Royal Engineer 1st Divn.

SUMMARY OF WORK PERFORMED BY R.E. UNITS 1st DIVISION.

From MIDDAY .... to Midday ....

Section.	Commanding Company.		Work carried out.					
I. OPERATIONS. (a).								
(b).								
(a).								
(b).								
II. INFORMATION.								
III. (a). Section "C" WORK.								
(b). Section "D"								
IV. WATER. (a). Section "C".								
(b). Section "D".								

Date ....

Rank.

1st DIVISION ENGINEERS DAILY PROGRESS REPORT.

FROM MID-DAY 23=4=15. TO MID-DAY 24=4=15.

Section.	Company.	
	26th Field Co.	2 Selections attached 3rd Coy R.E. Other Section preparing material.
	23rd Field Coy.	120' traverse (D line North of R.way) obtained and more built up. Further length of "B" dug out. Construction of both lines of bomb trench (re-entrant) advanced. Mule post fence trench erection commenced in front lines in front of CINDER TRACK. 2" traverse completed with traverses D line North of R.R.
	1st Lowland Fd. Coy.	On support trench from B line to no. 4 Bath. 3 traverses parapets & traverse over to sap heads — made bullet proof. Support of sap heads built to revetment height of 3'-0". On "D" line on North of Pas de Calais between B line + B line — dugouts to revetment height. Reached along "N.F.B" line to no. 4 sap. Cinder track leaving rails every 10 yds. Average length 7ft. C line to sap completed except for traverse, dugouts. Blown effects in orchard complete & to traverse built. Sap to No.11 L.O. almost complete 125 lineals. Preparation for overhead traverse chimney, loopholing, observation post (R.H.) Dug-outs for observation officers & traverses in front post shelters great. Repairs to King George road near RICHEBOURG. Splinter proof shelter behind traverses on North side of rue du bois & new work completed. Bomb proof at R.E. Store 3 completed.

24/4/1915.

Commanding

SUMMARY OF WORK PERFORMED BY R.E. UNITS 1st DIVISION.

From MIDDAY .... to midday ....

Section.	Company.	Work carried out.
I. OPERATIONS. (a).		
(b).		
(a).		
(b).		
II. INFORMATION.		
III. (a). Section "C" WORK.		
(b). Section "D".		
IV. WATER. (a). Section "C".		
(b). Section "D".		

Date ....   Rain. _____

1st DIVISION ENGINEERS DAILY PROGRESS REPORT.

FROM MID-DAY 22-4-15.   TO MID-DAY 23-4-15.

Section.	Company.	
	26th Field Co.	50' communication trench approximately 200' west of Bpre completed to 3'6" on top both sides, and sides in shelter places. Average 3'0". Dug-out about 8ft.
	23rd Field Coy.	Dug 120' of trench 6' deep, Avenue Roussillon in front of finished shelter dug-on left of factory square, which is held by R.E. Bien. Traverses needed on 6 line pridetrench, 50 yards per completion.
	1st Lowland Fd. Coy.	Communication trench from Kruisstraat, Kw. 14, South to Junction to top of curves, earthwork 120 yds. (ankle deep) thick 6/80 yds to top of curves & bullet proof parapet approximate to average 3ft. Raised freeboard of Plank 6' lane to average height of 2 ft. left bank of river. On line G Trenches 6 yards of Rue au Bois G. Parados completed Parados ... Parapet thickened - heightened, barbed wire between existing earthwork & new wire revetment. Demolition of factory chimney completed at Rue Croisette. Artillery observation post & party shelter being made. Two small bridges built over to widened & Hannebeek near 100m for P.O.C. 2-pounders proof shelters near G Bn in Brie Kebbit house, 6 lanes completed, 2 house commenced. 1 barricade between houses erected 4,000...

29/4/1915.

K. J. Wheeler, Major R.E.
for Commanding Roy Engr. 1st Division

SUMMARY OF WORK PERFORMED BY R.E. UNITS 1st DIVISION.

From MIDDAY .... to Midday ....

Section.	Company.	Work carried out.
I. OPERATIONS. (a).		
(b).		
(a).		
(b).		
II. INFORMATION.		
III. (a). Section "C" WORK.		
(b). Section "D"		
IV. WATER. (a). Section "C".		
(b). Section "D".		

Date ....

Rank.

1st DIVISION ENGINEERS DAILY PROGRESS REPORT.

FROM MID-DAY 21/4/15   TO MID-DAY 22/4/15

Company	Section	
26th Field Co.		
23rd Field Coy.	D.3.	Work in Con't Front leading from 3rd line breastwork to front breastwork used to put additional men on to filling sandbags with bricks & debris in 1st line breastwork & to lighten parts of breastwork. Material was weak in places. Breastwork at present also a magazine dwarf shelter, & that the height was increased in the wall. Thickening work here at the section and of the front trench.
	D.2.	All spandrels, loopholes & buttresses on west side Rue du Bois and 25' lengths behind breastworks completed.
1st Low-land Fd. Coy.	D.2.	Rue du trench from Peerstilly to new Epinette road in front due to heavy rain no further progress in firing could be made. About one hour & 1/4 length of trench (600 men) to be of heavy wooden flooring to be put in. Average thickness about 10' men also having no new carts ... Breastwork about 10 men & 50ed Braith Breastwork. I would go to 24 ... Require ... also heavy bricks ... & bridges for all roads. Consolidation of Breastwork Rue de ... Repairs to mud George Road & constructions continued at night. George road & ... at ... required to the chimney for bridge at September. ...
		Work on line B, night. Sent over the party to General Elliott's Engineer company breastwork, raising them to 4-6" making some failings of ...

22/4/1915.

for Commanding

SUMMARY OF WORK PERFORMED BY R&E. UNITS 1st DIVISION.

From MIDDAY .... to Midday ....

Section.	Company.	Work carried out.
I. OPERATIONS. (a).		
(b).		
(a).		
(b).		
II. INFORMATION.		
III. (a). Section "C" WORK.		
(b). Section "D"		
IV. WATER. (a). Section "C".		
(b). Section "D".		

Date ....

Rank ....

1st DIVISION ENGINEERS DAILY PROGRESS REPORT.

FROM MID-DAY 20=4=15.   TO MID-DAY 21=4=15.

Section.	Company.	
	26th Field Co.	
D.2.	23rd Field Coy.	60' new breastwork commenced in rear line N of Rue du Bois at an open space, this N/E corner. Breastwork running S.E. from N.E. corner of factory completed. Army trench parallel to + 120' due E of the Cinder track deepened at the N end, trench filled in behind traverses 15' & line entire length. Also knocking revetment + bullet proof traverses at alternate intervals of trench. 150' of breastwork new French communication trench under an Arrack approx 3 ft to front line 110° W.S.W. of the Cinder & road completed S.E. to front line 800° S.W./N.S.W copse completed & earth road C & I.F.
	1st Lowland Fd. Coy.	9 trestles erected in front of existing breastwork between Albert & between Street trenches at new place behind to heighten + build parapet. Repair to King George's Road & forward to Richebourg St. Vaast. Work continued on 3 enemy barb wire barbed wire fences in Rue du Bois between Albert & Edward Street, to be uncompleted fresh materials fetched to point. Not sufficient party. Every try so men. & other fences is completed even for the men on own trenches + to front C on N side of Rue du Bois, the pendants of Richelieu Manor corner moved to & & made bullet proof. New site of Rue du Bois between Albert & Edward roads. (continued)

21/4/1915.

for Commanding

SUMMARY OF WORK PERFORMED BY R.E. UNITS 1st DIVISION.

From MIDDAY .... to Midday ....

Section.	Company.	Work carried out.
I. OPERATIONS. (a).		
(b).		
(a).		
(b).		
II. INFORMATION.		
III. (a). Section "C" WORK.		
(b). Section "D"		
IV. WATER. (a). Section "C".		
(b). Section "D".		

Date ....

Rank ....

1st DIVISION ENGINEERS DAILY PROGRESS REPORT.

FROM MID-DAY 19=4=15.   TO MID-DAY 20=4=15.

Section.	Company.		
	26th Field Co.		Barbed wire entanglements & traverses. The following are completed:- N. of ST. FRANCOIS 1-10ft length. 1-25ft length. S-15ft length. N. of CHARITABLE 4-15ft length. 1-25ft length. 1-15ft length. New communication trench put E. of ST. FRANCOIS throughout, & covered with hurdles for 75ft. Traverse trench put E. of FARMY No.1 Rue de Bois, completed 30ft partly completed. 38ft Revetment E. of FARMY No.1 Rue de Bois completed & Roofed. Last 60ft of 90ft length of 200ft trench obtained.
D.1.	23rd Field Coy.		Work on life E to north side of Rue de Bois, & new screen parapets farmed N.E. of strong point leading across to west side of Rue at ALBERT ROAD. Some parapets between RICHOU & EDWARD AVES continued.
D.2.	1st Lowland Fd. Coy.		Repairs to King George Road at RICHEBOURG. Work continued in attaching new traverses to north side of RICHEBOURG between ALBERT & EDWARD AVES.

20/4/1915.

R.C.Maxwell Major R.E. [?] for
Cmg Engrs 1st Div.

Commanding

1st DIVISION ENGINEERS DAILY PROGRESS REPORT.

FROM MID-DAY 18·4·15 TO MID-DAY 19·4·15.

Company.	Section.	
26th Field Co.		Carried on work as last on Stables support trenches & Standing pits complete C.C. Bent storage over hitch in Rue de Bois. Communt trench just E. of Rd dug to depth 3'6" to 4'6" from surface, with 25cm trench across part, trench 3 feet wide, front line—with parapet breastwork now complete between S.a. + Rd. T.6.
23rd Field Co.	F.D. 2.	Y.O. reconnoitred an emergency trench to Rue T.6. S.O.A. reconnoitred to commandant breastwork with communication to Rd T.6. Filler completed.
1st Lowland Fd. Coy.	II SECTION	The Section Commander with 15 sappers & 20 [?] of 2/K.R.R. worked from 2a.m. until 5a.m. on Breastwork S4 [?] constructed about 40 yards. Instructed up to [?] height 3'6" B.K. Rpd 11th Div R.E. N.A. + R.B. Repaired 25 King George Road up to Rue du Chasseurs at RICHEBOURG. No [?] [?] [?] between Ruits N + S. 35 yards of 4'-6" concrete laterally. [?] [?] [?] finished [?] [?] [?] [?] [?] [?]. [?] from Conseil [?] [?] [?] [?] [?] [?] to station N.E. [?] 600 sandbags sent to [?] [?] [?] for breastwork of [?] [?] [?] [?] [?] [?] and [?] [?] [?] [?] between N.W. [?] of 10th of 4th report moved back [?] by a
D.T.		
		distance of 10 yds. Breastwork raised to average height of 3'0"

19/4/1915.

[signature]

Lieut R.A. for
Maj Engnr 1st Div
Commanding

SUMMARY OF WORK PERFORMED BY R&E. UNITS 1st DIVISION.

From MIDDAY .... to Midday ....

Section.	Company.	Work carried out.
I. OPERATIONS. (a).		
(b).		
(a).		
(b).		
II. INFORMATION.		
III. (a). Section "C". WORK.		
(b). Section "D".		
IV. WATER. (a). Section "C".		
(b). Section "D".		

Date ....

Rain. ....

1st DIVISION ENGINEERS DAILY PROGRESS REPORT.

FROM MID-DAY 14=4=15.   TO MID-DAY 15=4=15.

Section.	Company.	
	26th Field Coy.	Carried on work on splinter proofs & traverses on breastworks in rear line. 30 traverses begun & completed to 1'-6", with 1'-6" over, i.e. 1'6"x 1'6" overall way. Wing platforms N of Rue de Bois 75 manhours. Front part E of fleury completed. New loopholes and sentry posts commenced. Front line breastwork between Ruts 6a & 6 completed. 18 hours. Sentry posts & parapet breastwork with notch to H Coy's trench reported.
	23rd Field Coy.	Reported to King George's Road RICHEBOURG. Bn near front line trenches — Nieuw Burth 2+3, - B+4, +parapet being raised to new front line trenches - Nieuw Burth 4+6 work of raising & thickening under front to pass — to Communication trench from Intge Rs. to Ruts 6. 54 Thunderers erected. Passage raised to 4'-6" for another 80 yds — for another 30 yds completed raised & iron work or splinter proof. Stubben Aubert & Edward Road continued. Loop-holes over the trench in rear of SP.
	1st Lowland Fd. Coy.	In Rue de Bois (N near), Gaps 4.30 yds turfed & wire raised to SP. Gap of 50 yds between and shift into breastworks joined up. Earthwork made to key bridge of 3-8'.

1/1915.

SS Gilbert Capt. R.E.
Commanding 1 Coy. Engrs. 1st Div.

SUMMARY OF WORK PERFORMED BY R.&E. UNITS 1st DIVISION.

From MIDDAY .... to Midday ....

Section.	Company.	Work carried out.
I. OPERATIONS. (a).		
(b).		
(a).		
(b).		
II. INFORMATION.		
III. (a). Section "C" WORK.		
(b). Section "D".		
IV. WATER. (a). Section "C".		
(b). Section "D".		

Date .... Rain. ....

1st DIVISION ENGINEERS DAILY PROGRESS REPORT.

FROM MID-DAY 16=4=15" TO MID-DAY 17=4=15".

Section.	Company.	
	26th Field Co.	Obtained & fixed in site 100 hurdles for breastwork of VERTOIS, wire & portion of this revetment to pickets & commence earthwork.
	23rd Field Coy.	Work continued on observation stations & splinter proof shelters for same. Sites for Listening Posts for intruding chosen & work on same begun. 35' new breastwork east of Butt 5 revetted & completed.
D.2.	1st Lowland Fd. Coy.	Work on breastwork between Butt 4 & 5 — abandoned hoping it earthen which 40' to left of Butt 4 (as far as bridge over ditch) to height of 4 ft. Repairing KING GEORGE'S ROAD, RICHEBOURG. Communication trench from INDIAN line to Butt 5, hurdles erected for distance of 170'. Earth thrown up to height of 4ft & rivetted. Work continued on quantity proofing, behind houses on Rue de l'Epinette about & beyond road, beginning repairs to improvised front with sandbags. It would perhaps ensure it perhaps permanently repaired.

17/4/1915.

Commanding Engineer, 1st Division

SUMMARY OF WORK PERFORMED BY R&E. UNITS 1st DIVISION.

From MIDDAY .... to Midday ....

Section.	Company.	Work carried out.
I. OPERATIONS. (a).		
(b).		
(a).		
(b).		
II. INFORMATION.		
III. (a). Section "C" WORK.		
(b). Section "D"		
IV. WATER. (a). Section "C".		
(b). Section "D".		

Date ....

Rain.

1st DIVISION ENGINEERS DAILY PROGRESS REPORT.

FROM MID-DAY 15=4=15   TO MID-DAY 16=4=15

Section.	Company.	
	26th Field Co.	Resting.
D.1.	23rd Field Coy.	55' breastwork erected between Butts 5+6. 44' of revetting to Coys trench leading to Butt 6, made & put. 3 Observation stations commenced & thinking at open parts of communications N/f Rue De Bois carried out.
D.2.	1st Lowland Fd. Coy.	Work on new breastwork between Butts 4+5: Gap filled in, cow ditch - breastwork on brige built with revetting to height of 5ft. Carried to average height of 3-0ft for 10 x behind new trestles. 23 ft. to complete. Repairs to KING GEORGES ROAD, RUE DU BOIS. Trench cut across road & pipes laid to drain ditch alongside road.
		New breastwork between Butts 10 & 11. Raised & made bullet proof. Bridge built over ditch at machine gun emplacement & screen f existing wicker or Parapet between 10 D + 10 E heightened & strengthened in places where it had sunk. Water tight fences started in front trench between Sutherland Avenue.
		Cover position made with sandbags f earth overhead cover in rear of houses on North Side of RUE DE BOIS between ALBERT ROAD & EDWARD ROAD.

16-14-/1915.

F.C. Whiting
Commanding Royl. Engrs. 1st Divn.

SUMMARY OF WORK PERFORMED BY R.E. UNITS 1st DIVISION.

From MIDDAY .... to Midday ....

Section.	Company.	Work carried out.
I. OPERATIONS. (a).		
(b).		
(a).		
(b).		
II. INFORMATION.		
III. (a). Section "C" WORK.		
(b). Section "D"		
IV. WATER. (a). Section "C".		
(b). Section "D".		

Date ....

_____
Rank.

1st DIVISION ENGINEERS DAILY PROGRESS REPORT.

FROM MID-DAY 14=4=15   TO MID-DAY 15=4=15

Section.	Company.	
(?)	26th Field Co.	Resting.
23rd	Field Coy.	16" across Advanced post. 40" cover erected on access French from BURLINGTON ARCH OB to front line. 80' new trench completed west of Rout 6.
D.2.	1st Lowland Fd. Coy.	Repairs to 9 men shelters near RICHEBOURG. Parapets heightened & thickened between Ruits 1 + 2; 3 traverses made. Parapet heightened & thickened between Ruits 1 + 10½. 2 traverses made. Machine Gun emplacement built between Ruits 3 + 4. Parapet our Ewret (w/Lewis) across from 2'0 to 5'0". Breastwork, inside 1 firearms, to be 4' 6" for a distance of 30'.

15/4/1915.

[signature] Lieut. R.E. for

[signature]
Commanding Roy. Eng's. 1st D.V.

SUMMARY OF WORK PERFORMED BY R&E. UNITS 1st DIVISION.

From MIDDAY .... to Midday ....

Section.	Company.	Work carried out.
I. OPERATIONS. (a).		
(b).		
(a).		
(b).		
II. INFORMATION.		
III. (a). Section "C" WORK.		
(b). Section "D"		
IV. WATER. (a). Section "C".		
(b). Section "D".		

Date ....

Rank.

1st DIVISION ENGINEERS DAILY PROGRESS REPORT.

FROM MID-DAY 13-4-15.   TO MID-DAY 14-4-15.

Section.	Company.	
	26th Field Co.	Resting
	23rd Field Coy.	33' of new trestle complete between Poplar & the Pont Orient R. Coy. M. Coy. R. Coy. from Burlington Arcade 6 p.m. Also employed placing floats for bridge & small bridges. Infantry had orders on putting up frames 200 behind trestle.
	1st Lowland Fd. Coy.	Section engaged completing drainage going to R.E. compound. Rapport Avenue by & loading of a distance of 10 feet also M.G. emplacement finished and turfed. Pavement 11 of per round wire entanglement 3 lengths of 2 X 4 dug in panels below one across the Coy Road & rock used. Trenches renewing. No.2 Section finished RG of R.E dug outs near Cople Orchard. Dug outs being completed 3 x 6 x 6 & 2 and 2 3 sandbag round & revetted. Finish turfed. No.3 Section tr of elsewhere thrown up in front of Lovers Avenue. Right Coy 3.6 panels one deep.

14/4/1915.

Commanding Roy. Engrs. 1st Divn.

SUMMARY OF WORK PERFORMED BY R&E. UNITS 1st DIVISION.

From MIDDAY .... to Midday ....

Section.	Company.	Work carried out.
I. OPERATIONS. (a).		
(b).		
(a).		
(b).		
II. INFORMATION.		
III. (a). Section "C" WORK.		
(b). Section "D".		
IV. WATER. (a). Section "C".		
(b). Section "D".		

Date .... Rain. ....

1st DIVISION ENGINEERS DAILY PROGRESS REPORT.

FROM MID-DAY 12=4-15   TO MID-DAY 13-4-15

Section.	Company.	
E.3.	26th Field Coy.	CHATEAU KEEP completed. HILLS REDOUBT completed except communication trench 3 wire which troops to making with. CHURCH KEEP. all traverses completed, wire completed & wrought iron sheets all completed over frame in position. Lightly covered with earth. The whole section handed over in detail to Maj. Thurston R.E. & coy Sappers 9th Indian Division.
D.2.	23rd Field Coy.	40' new breastwork completed west of Redt 6. Deepened + 10' ft. lowered 95' communication trench to breastwork west of Redt 6.
	1st Lowland Fd. Coy.	95 wire entanglement frames erected in front of breastwork redt 4 & 9 about 300yds. Two completed the wiring of front from Junc Redt. 10 right flank D.1 Section. Repairs to RICHEBOURG new front line breastwork between Redts 1 & 2. Emplacement between 10' & 21' Redt finished. New notice Boards erected on houses in Indian Village:- THIS HOUSE IS MI[...] Bearing ditches near Indian village.

13/4/1915.

Major R.E. for
Commanding Major Sapp. & Min.

1st DIVISION ENGINEERS DAILY PROGRESS REPORT.

FROM MID-DAY 11=4=15.   TO MID-DAY 12=4=15.

Section.	Company.	
F.3.	26th Field Co.	HILL REDOUBT. Church entrance – Embrasures cut. French improvement – Wire entanglements bayonets on sough the enemy. CHURCH REDOUBT. 1 bay S.W. & new cross fire 2 ups superstructure.
D.3	23rd Field Coy.	Bought 4 P.S. of Hyponeristies leave bridge loaded to R.E. Stores. 10' Communication trench N. of bridge incised in enemy's inspected to S.E.T. 50 yards trench completed joining 136 & P.R. 1 Scrape deepened with carried. Bar kept by head & Sappers.
	1st Lowland Fd. Coy.	Repair to road near R.E. Dump completed. High temporary road (?) & wire to enable heavy guns to pass over is finished R.E. Later. Priming & clearing away debris at site of new post destroyed E. of R.E. Dump. Parapet of Keep Redoubt (H.L.I. section) raised to average height of 3'11" for 10 yds.

12/4/1915.   [signature] Major R.E.
Commanding 1st Div Engineers

SUMMARY OF WORK PERFORMED BY R.&E. UNITS 1st DIVISION.

From MIDDAY .... to Midday ....

Section.	Company.	Work carried out.								
I. OPERATIONS. (a).										
(b).										
(a).										
(b).										
II. INFORMATION.										
III. (a). Section "C" WORK.										
(b). Section "D".										
IV. WATER. (a). Section "C".										
(b). Section "D".										

Date ....

Said.

1st DIVISION ENGINEERS DAILY PROGRESS REPORT.

FROM MID-DAY 10=4=15. TO MID-DAY 11=4=15.

Section.	Company.	
E.3.	26th Field Co.	CHATEAU REDOUBT, completed except for work inside house, which will be done in course of any. CHURCH KEEP. Parapet and banquette narrowed. Hoping completed except for overhead cover. This is quite complete & excepting communication trench, and sides of new communication trench completed.
	23rd Field Coy.	36 ft of new trenchwork completed east of P.R. Hope to connect this with 8 ft to night. 17ft traverse on left of R.P. 6 bridge over a form in an ammm approx. Mine bridges under construction.
	1st Lowland Fd. Coy.	New front line trenches between houses built & 9/100 near redt No 1. 145 yds in rows W-6 ft sap & 4 will support ws/sh of machine gun emplacement. Parapet between R.5 & Rolls — thread topen parapet on left side of communication trench from Royal house & Orchard. 2 machine gun emplacement being made hereby for true but extra head cover strewn up infront. Trenches opened between 23 & 4 Redts 1'-6" each strewn up infront. Ramp to front near RICHEBOURG — making new emplacement formin. Clearing top surface of P.A. Howitzer foundation.

11/4/1915.

Ivanston Major R.E. for
Commanding Roy. Engr. 1st Div.

SUMMARY OF WORK PERFORMED BY R.&E. UNITS 1st DIVISION.

From MIDDAY .... to Midday ....

Section.	Company.	Work carried out.
I. OPERATIONS. (a).		
(b).		
(a).		
(b).		
II. INFORMATION.		
III. (a). Section "C" WORK.		
(b). Section "D".		
IV. WATER. (a). Section "C".		
(b). Section "D".		

Date............................   Rain.

1st DIVISION ENGINEERS DAILY PROGRESS REPORT.

FROM MID-DAY 9=4=15.   TO MID-DAY 10=4=15.

Section.	Company.	
	26th Field Coy.	STATION REDOUBT. overhead cover & parapets completed — 6 traps of loopholes — work remaining is overhead cover inside, & alterations & new gun emplacement details. CHURCH REDOUBT. parapet & range of loopholes completed on E. S. & W. sides & parados in N. flooring nearly completed & materials for overhead cover gotten in. HILLS REDOUBT. parados commenced & alterations & supports of communication trench marked out & commenced, & emplacement altered & supports
	23rd Field Coy.	30 × new traverses completed. Part of corner trench & 6 × mat-90 × " " checkered. trench machine gun S. gas alley &c. &c. (new work) started opening up. 4. Bridges laid down and a road cut in front of approx barrier on road to left of 25 for M.H.
	1st Lowland Fd. Coy.	New front line trenches left of Grove Butt to direction of drain Butt completed for 120 yds 4'-6" × 3'-6" thick. Repair to row near Rickaburg trench. 89 knife rest wire entanglement in front of new front line trenches between Post A & right of Post 9, a distance of 180y.

10/4/1915.   Hindson
              1 Coy. Engr. p. 25.

                        Commanding
                        Hindson 1 Coy. Engr. p. 25.

SUMMARY OF WORK PERFORMED BY R&E. UNITS 1st DIVISION.

From MIDDAY .... to Midday ....

Section.	Company.	Work carried out.
I. OPERATIONS. (a).		
(b).		
(a).		
(b).		
II. INFORMATION.		
III. (a). Section "C" WORK.		
(b). Section "D".		
IV. WATER. (a). Section "C".		
(b). Section "D".		

Date .... Rank.

1st DIVISION. ENGINEERS DAILY PROGRESS REPORT.

FROM MID-DAY 7=4=15.   TO MID-DAY 9=4=15.

Section.	Company.	
E.3.	26th Field Co.	CHURCH REDOUBT. - parapet built up with sandbags but half parapet completed - number of sandbags used - 3500 - loopholes are opened and cleared. HILL REDOUBT. - No dugouts unfinished. - left arm of right redoubt improving the trench are completed and left completed and sandbags. Communication trench up to right redoubt from NW corner opened. Loopholes along ordinary line. NEW MACHINE gun embrasure.
	23rd Field Coy.	40 × new traverses completed in A & F.P.1. Shrine or line on left of F.P. was consequently occupied by the alarm of attack.
	1st Lowland Fd. Coy.	Repairs to road near RICHEBOURG. Forward road between Grand Rullek & Indian Belt - overseer to 6" high. Full road at part L. & reminder raised to average height 3'-0". Compressor machine & our employment. All communication trench leading to Gun shelter enclosed at front line in front of trenches. Please see Sapper engineer to Commandant forward to reinstate new line needed from part K.C. In light of the alarm in the night.

Commanding Roy Engrs

9/4/1915.

1st DIVISION ENGINEERS DAILY PROGRESS REPORT.

FROM MID-DAY 7=4=15 TO MID-DAY 8=4=15

Section.	Company.		
F.3.	26th Field Co.	Station Records. 3 bays overhead cover completed. 27yds. Parados to Traverses completed, overhead cover & Parados is now complete except for about length at entrance. NEUVE CHAPELLE. New track from CHIMNEY CRESCENT now except from CARTS REDOUBT to Main Chapelle excellent - Drains cleaned.	
	23rd Field Coy.	26' french flecked with ladders & piers fit 6' waterway. 15' french pulaurier & revetmt to 4'-6" made overhead this portion of trench to house the sharp bend. 40 to 50 yds from the Lt of P.S & face S.F. 30' breastwork erected between P.1 + P.2 - 2 loopholes even in breastwork just E. of old Com.t Trench near P.1 2 Traverses so arranged (complete) just west of old Com.t trench near P.1 & breastwork between P.1 breastwork & old loophole.	
D.L.	1st Lowland Fd. Coy.	Erected 16 hurdles & brought up trenchwork to a height of 4'6" by 3' average thickness. 2½ gns of new front line breastwork left of Chemin Boute E. (4'6" Inf.t working party available). Completed Loopholing of breastwork between Orchard Redt. & Genies Redt E. & Filled up holes in height of 3' for 45'. Repair to house near RICHE BOURG. Preparation of 50 the Inclosetment frames & tarpaulins etc.	

Maurice Major R.E. for
Commanding Roy. Engr. 1st Div.

8/4/1915.

SUMMARY OF WORK PERFORMED BY R&E. UNITS 1st DIVISION.

From MIDDAY .... to Midday ....

Section.	Company.	Work carried out.
I. OPERATIONS. (a).		
(b).		
(a).		
(b).		
II. INFORMATION.		
III. (a). Section "C" WORK.		
(b). Section "D"		
IV. WATER. (a). Section "C".		
(b). Section "D".		

Date .... R.E.

1st DIVISION ENGINEERS DAILY PROGRESS REPORT.

FROM MID-DAY 6=4=15" TO MID-DAY 7=4=15"

Section.	Company.	
	26th Field Co.	Work continued on CHATEAU and CHURCH REDOUBTS inner nearly completed, latter being strong. Wire entanglement through NEUVE CHAPELLE nearly finished. Work on CHATEAU-REDOUBT delayed by chiefs of congratulation and chiefs of congratulation.
	23rd Field Coy.	(1) East of P.S. work on repairs & renewed revelation habitable. (2) 30* new breastwork complete east of P.1. (3) Int. carrying party thickening 90* of breastwork east of P.1.
	1st Lowland Fd. Coy.	Repairs to trench near RICHEBOURG. Erected 3.2 hurdles on new front line breastwork between Rue du Bois & Croix Barbée. Erected 103 knife rest wire entanglement frames from Post 10 to 15. 50 x night of Post 10 P.4 advance of 200 yds. Preparation of knife rest wire entanglement frames.

7.4. /1915.

.... Arundel Major R.E. for
Commanding 1 Coy. Engr. 1st Div.

SUMMARY OF WORK PERFORMED BY R&E. UNITS 1st DIVISION.

From MIDDAY .... to Midday ....

Section.	Company.	Work carried out.
I. OPERATIONS. (a).		
(b).		
(a).		
(b).		
II. INFORMATION.		
III. (a). Section "C" WORK.		
(b). Section "D".		
IV. WATER. (a). Section "C".		
(b). Section "D".		

Date ....

Rank.

1st DIVISION ENGINEERS DAILY PROGRESS REPORT.

FROM MID-DAY 3=4=15. TO MID-DAY 6=5=15.

Section.	Company.		
	26th Field Co.	CHATEAU REDOUBT with an overhead cover now finished. NEUVE CHAPELLE 66" north wire fence 80" single wire fence completed, previous fence traces & improved. CHURCH REDOUBT, parapet now completed. HILL 5 REDOUBT wire now being completed.
	23rd Field Coy.	90" of breastwork erected to 4'6" height completed (Sap D 3 Left P) E. Section 1 bay (10") completed E. of P.S. 2 bays (20") erected to an average of 3' Roofs of all 3 bays laid with sandbags.
	1st Lowland Fd. Coy.	Preparing knife rests now in enlargement frames. Repairing road near RICHEBOURG owing to heavy rain last night but in the time little trouble was expected.

6/4/1915.

[signature] Krumm
Commanding Royal Engineers 1st Division.

SUMMARY OF WORK PERFORMED BY R.&E. UNITS 1st DIVISION.

From MIDDAY .... to Midday ....

Section.	Company.	Work carried out.
I. OPERATIONS. (a).		
(b).		
(a).		
(b).		
II. INFORMATION.		
III. (a). Section "C" WORK.		
(b). Section "D".		
IV. WATER. (a). Section "C".		
(b). Section "D".		

Date ....

R.E.

1st DIVISION ENGINEERS DAILY PROGRESS REPORT.

FROM MID-DAY 4=4=15. TO MID-DAY 5=4=15.

Section.	Company.		
(1) Engrs. in NEUVE CHAPELLE	26th Field Co.	Continued work on HILL'S REDOUBT, & CHATEAU REDOUBT, constructing dug-outs in former & overhead cover in latter case. Continued wiring streets in NEUVE CHAPELLE.	
D	23rd Field Coy.	(1) 40' fresh work completed to P.1. (2) 90' of 2'6" × 2' bench dug east of P.1. (3) 85' trench revetting done and made new hurdle east of P.5.	
D.2.	1st Lowland Fd. Coy.	78 hurdles erected between Group Redt E. & Indians and also advanced engagements. Tracing of new front line N.v. Repairs to wire near RICHEBOURG preceding Redt E & Indian line. More entanglement frames between RedtE & Indian line. Water gauge readings: {Wtrn H.Q. — 7 no change {E.3 Redent 17} no change	Pierre E'Mch. — 3½ Choura Phocher + ½ Rout P.A. + ½	24 hrs / ones P.M. — ½ — ½

5/4/1915.

H. Winston Major R.E.

Commanding Roy. Engrs. 1st Division.

SUMMARY OF WORK PERFORMED BY R&E. UNITS 1st DIVISION.

From MIDDAY .... to Midday ....

Section.	Company.	Work carried out.
I. OPERATIONS. (a).		
(b).		
(a).		
(b).		
II. INFORMATION.		
III. (a). Section "C" WORK.		
(b). Section "D".		
IV. WATER. (a). Section "C".		
(b). Section "D".		

Date ....

Rank ....

1st DIVISION ENGINEERS DAILY PROGRESS REPORT.

FROM MID-DAY 3=4=15 TO MID-DAY 4=4=15

Section.	Company.	
E.	26th Field Co.	CHATEAU REDOUBT. 3 bays finished - sandbag revetting - 3 bays of parapet complete on S. side. - 15 yds sandbag wall parados on E. side. NEUVE CHAPELLE. No yds trench here completed - previous crew shortened - 30 yds wire very big chevaux-de-frise erected covering crew from G.L.4 hills REDOUBT & dugouts completed, nearly completed - new long communication trench 3 parapet cover good finished - wire round M.G. emplacement. Communication trench though parapet cover good.
D.2 & 3	23rd Field Coy.	35' frontwork E. of hilt to be completed. 44' of old french E. of point 5' raised such ladders.
D.1.	1st Lowland Fd. Coy.	water level risen 1". Communication trenches from Bomb House 16 Guins Ruin E. Chicoserv parapet. bad side for works were filth. Several small pieces of parapet near Att. H. support trench along 9" for 25 yds near ditch. Somewhere two screenway posts bad side near Bomb House. Commenced boring up to dam/Ritz with house suite E. trench in whole length aboveground 1'0"/1'6". Represents near RICHEBOURG. Water gauge readings. (1'5a H.Q. E.3 Rinault

24 letters | Siren 6" Mat | Siren 3/3 Cheveuse 6 et | | |
-3¾	+¼	-¾
no change	Pont S.A. +¼	+¼ = -⅜
		+6

Major R.E. for
C.R.E. 1st Division.

Commanding

4/4/1915.

1st DIVISION ENGINEERS DAILY PROGRESS REPORT.

FROM MID-DAY 2=4=15.   TO MID-DAY 3=4=15.

Section.	Company.	
F.	26th Field Co.	CHATEAU REDOUBT overhead cover nearly half finished. CHURCH " " " wiring where not finished continued on parapet, wiring of line from Chateau Redoubt for 190x nearly completed.
	23rd Field Coy.	30x of breastworks to the left of Redoubt completed as men to continue revision & complete communication traverses with owner.
D.1. D.2 & 3.	1st Lowland Fd. Coy.	Communication trench from Rouge Maison to Breastwork - Sections along and complete hurdles all the way to B.13 up & earthed to average thickness of 2'-6" at top. Regt dine. 23 hurdles placed from R'douit to breastwork in front line or right of INDIAN VILLAGE complete. New front line between N & M. Raised to 4'-6" for 70x to make good gap to left of Post & filled up with sandbags to height of 5-6' to take breastwork for 5/60x on each side of gap completed.

3/4/1915.

Wright
Major R.E.
for Commanding Roy. Engrs. 1st Divn.

1st DIVISION ENGINEERS DAILY PROGRESS REPORT.

FROM MID-DAY 1=4=15   TO MID-DAY 2=4=15

Section.	Company.	
	26th Field Co.	Work continued on FIELD REDOUBT, TRENCH REDOUBT & CHATEAU REDOUBT. Three new men reported in D.R. Dn & have taken over HILLS REDOUBT & the enclosed area.
	23rd Field Coy.	Continued work on L.D. & C.T. from Line Farm to CAPPER'S Ro. Rd. of southward sub to RUE SYLV. R.T. Continued from trench dug down Essex Road.
	1st Lowland Fd. Coy.	Reconnoit'd finished Line two. TROKN VILLAGE no 1 type & b.b. & bb. Connects hand from BRASS HOUSE. A WIRE supplies ho hostlert ? between 10th & 10th exp?bhs? remember to ? ? ? them at Brig-room HQ of P.Q area. Full? high Field. ?

2/4/1915.

(signature)
Maj. R.E. for
Comg Eng 1st Dvn.

Commanding

SUMMARY OF WORK PERFORMED BY R&E. UNITS 1st DIVISION.

From MIDDAY .... to Midday ....

Section.	Company.	Work carried out.
I. OPERATIONS. (a).-		
(b).-		
(a).-		
(b).-		
II. INFORMATION.		
III. (a).- Section "C". WORK.		
(b).- Section "D".		
IV. WATER. (a). Section "C".		
(b). Section "D".		

Date .... Rain. ....

www.ingramcontent.com/pod-product-compliance
Lightning Source LLC
Chambersburg PA
CBHW081355160426
43192CB00013B/2416